# Traction

## A STARTUP GUIDE
## TO GETTING CUSTOMERS

Gabriel Weinberg and Justin Mares

BUSINESS
HD
62.5
.W45
2014g

ISBN 978-0976339601

# Table of Contents

# Traction Trumps Everything

Building a successful company is hard. Really hard. We've been involved in both startup successes and startup failures.

Who are we? Gabriel is currently the CEO and founder of DuckDuck-Go, an alternative search engine he started in 2008 that received over a billion searches in 2013 and is growing rapidly. In 2006, he sold his last company, Opobox, for ten million. Gabriel is also an active angel investor, having invested in over ten early stage ventures with two successful exits so far.

Justin founded two startups (one of which was acquired) and recently ran growth at Exceptional Cloud Services, which was acquired by Rackspace in 2013.

Traction is the best way to improve your chances of startup success. Traction is a sign that something is working. If you charge for your product, it means customers are buying. If your product is free, it's a growing userbase.

Traction is powerful. Technical, market, and team risks are easier to address with traction. Fundraising, hiring, press, partnerships and acquisitions are all easier with traction.

In other words, *traction trumps everything*.

This book is for startups of all kinds: consumer or enterprise-focused, from ecommerce to apps and everything in between.

We've interviewed more than forty founders, studied many more companies, and pulled out the repeatable strategies and tactics they used to succeed.

Our goal is to show you how to get traction no matter what business you're in.

# CHAPTER 1

# Traction Channels

Before we get started, let's define what traction is. Traction is a sign that your company is taking off. It's obvious in your core metrics: if you have a mobile app, your download rate is growing rapidly. If you're a search engine, your number of searches is skyrocketing. If a SaaS tool, your monthly revenue is blowing up. If a consumer app, your daily active users are increasing quickly. You get the point.

Naval Ravikant, founder of AngelList, an online platform that helps companies raise money, says it well:

*"Traction is basically quantitative evidence of customer demand. So if you're in enterprise software, [initial traction] may be two or three early customers who are paying a bit; if you're in consumer software the bar might be as high as hundreds of thousands of users. ... It's the Supreme Court definition of porn. You'll know it when you see it."*

You can always get more traction. The whole point of a startup is to grow rapidly. Getting traction means moving your growth curve up and to the right as best you can. Paul Graham, founder of startup accelerator Y Combinator, puts it like this:

*"A startup is a company designed to grow fast. Being newly founded does not in itself make a company a startup. Nor is it necessary for a startup to work on technology, or take venture funding, or have some sort of 'exit.' The only essential thing is growth. Everything else we associate with startups follows from growth."*

In other words, **traction is growth. The pursuit of traction is what defines a startup**.

## Nineteen Traction Channels

After interviewing more than forty successful founders and researching countless more, we discovered that **startups get traction through nineteen different channels**. Many successful startups experimented with multiple channels (search engine marketing, business development, etc.) until they found one that worked.

We call these customer acquisition channels *traction channels*. These are marketing and distribution channels through which your startup can get traction: real users and customers.

We discovered two broad themes through our research:

1. Most founders only consider using traction channels they're already familiar with or think they should be using because of their type of product or company. This means that **far too many startups focus on the same channels** (search engine marketing, public relations) and ignore other promising ways to get traction.

2. It's hard to predict the channel that will work best. You can make educated guesses, but **until you start running tests, it's difficult to tell which channel is the *best* one for you right now**.

Our introductory chapters 2–5 expand on these themes. Chapter 2 introduces our Bullseye Framework for getting traction. Essentially, it involves targeted experimentation with a few traction channels, followed by laser focus on the one that is working.

Chapters 3 and 4 offer traction strategies and tactics to apply when using Bullseye, including pursuing traction development in parallel with product development. Chapter 5 offers one way to approach parallel traction/product development – called the Critical Path – where you focus on a single traction goal and ignore everything not required to achieve it.

Before you jump into this material, however, we'd like to introduce you to the nineteen traction channels and some of the people we interviewed for them. We will explore each of these channels in chapters 6–24.

When going through these traction channels try your best not to dismiss them as irrelevant for your company. **Each traction channel has worked for startups of all kinds and in all different stages**. Get one channel working that your competitors dismiss, and you can grow rapidly while they languish.

## Viral Marketing (Chapter 6)

Viral marketing consists of growing your userbase by encouraging your users to refer other users. We interviewed Andrew Chen, a viral marketing expert and mentor at 500 Startups, for common viral techniques and the factors that have led to viral adoption in major startups. We also talked with Ashish Kundra of myZamana, who discussed using viral marketing to grow from 100k users to over 4 million in less than a year.

## Public Relations (Chapter 7)

Public relations (PR) is the art of getting your name out there via traditional media outlets like newspapers, magazines and TV. We interviewed Jason Kincaid, former TechCrunch writer, about pitching media outlets, how to form relationships with reporters, and what most startups do wrong when it comes to PR. We also talked with Ryan Holiday, bestselling author of *Trust Me, I'm Lying* and media strategist, to learn how startups could leverage today's rapidly changing media landscape to get traction.

**Unconventional PR (Chapter 8)**

Unconventional PR involves doing something exceptional (like publicity stunts) to draw media attention. This channel can also work by repeatedly going above and beyond for your customers. Alexis Ohanian told us some of the things he did to get (and keep) people talking about reddit and Hipmunk, two startups he co-founded.

**Search Engine Marketing (Chapter 9)**

Search engine marketing (SEM) allows companies to advertise to consumers searching on Google and other search engines. We interviewed Matthew Monahan of Inflection, the company behind Archives.com (before its $100 million acquisition by Ancestry.com) to learn how Archives relied primarily on SEM for their growth.

**Social and Display Ads (Chapter 10)**

Ads on popular sites like reddit, YouTube, Facebook, Twitter and hundreds of other niche sites can be a powerful and scalable way to reach new customers. We brought in Nikhil Sethi, founder of the social ad buying platform Adaptly, to talk with us about getting traction with social and display ads.

**Offline Ads (Chapter 11)**

Offline ads include TV spots, radio commercials, billboards, infomercials, newspaper and magazine ads, as well as flyers and other local advertisements. These ads reach demographics that are harder to target online, like seniors, less tech-savvy consumers and commuters. Few startups use this channel, which means there's less competition for many of these audiences. We talked with Jason Cohen, founder of WPEngine and Smart Bear Software, about the offline ads he's used to acquire customers.

**Search Engine Optimization (Chapter 12)**

Search engine optimization (SEO) is the process of making sure your website shows up for key search results. We interviewed Rand Fishkin of Moz (the market leader in SEO software) to talk about best practices for getting traction with SEO.

Patrick McKenzie, founder of Appointment Reminder, also explained to us how he uses SEO to cheaply acquire lots of highly targeted traffic.

### Content Marketing (Chapter 13)

Many startups have blogs. However, most don't use their blogs to get traction. We talked with Rick Perreault, founder of Unbounce, and OkCupid founder Sam Yagan to learn how their blogs transformed their businesses.

### Email Marketing (Chapter 14)

Email marketing is one of the best ways to convert prospects while retaining and monetizing existing ones. For this chapter we interviewed Colin Nederkoorn, founder of email marketing startup Customer.io, to discuss how startups can get the most out this traction channel.

### Engineering as Marketing (Chapter 15)

Using engineering resources to acquire customers is an underutilized way to get traction. Successful companies have built micro-sites, developed widgets, and created free tools that drive thousands of leads each month. We asked Dharmesh Shah, founder of Hubspot, to discuss how engineering as marketing has driven Hubspot's growth to tens of thousands of customers through tools like their Marketing Grader.

### Targeting Blogs (Chapter 16)

Popular startups like Codecademy, Mint, and reddit all got their start by targeting blogs. Noah Kagan, Mint's former director of marketing, told us how he targeted niche blogs early on, and how this strategy allowed Mint to acquire 40,000 users before launching.

### Business Development (Chapter 17)

Business development (BD) is the process of creating strategic relationships that benefit both your startup and your partner. Paul English, co-founder and CEO of Kayak.com, walked us through the impact of their early partnership with AOL. We also interviewed venture capitalist Chris Fralic, whose BD efforts at Half.com were a major factor in eBay's $350 million acquisition of the company.

We'll show you how to structure deals, find strategic partners, build a business development pipeline, and approach potential partners.

## Sales (Chapter 18)

Sales is primarily focused on creating processes to directly exchange product for dollars. We interviewed David Skok of Matrix Partners – someone who's taken four different companies public – to get his perspective on how the best software companies are creating sustainable, scalable sales processes. We also take a look at how to find early customers and have winning sales conversations.

## Affiliate Programs (Chapter 19)

Companies like Hostgator, GoDaddy and Sprout Social have robust affiliate programs that have allowed them to reach hundreds of thousands of customers in a cost-effective way. We interviewed Kristopher Jones, founder of the Pepperjam Affiliate network, to learn how a startup can leverage this channel. We also talked with Maneesh Sethi to learn how affiliate marketers choose what products to promote, and some of the strategies they use to do so.

## Existing Platforms (Chapter 20)

Focusing on existing platforms means focusing your growth efforts on a mega-platform like Facebook, Twitter, or an App Store and getting some of their hundreds of millions of users to use your product. Alex Pachikov, co-founder of Evernote, explained how their focus on Apple's App Store generated millions of customers.

## Trade Shows (Chapter 21)

Trade shows are a chance for companies in specific industries to show off their latest products. We interviewed Brian Riley of SlidePad, an innovative bike brake startup, to learn how they sealed a partnership that led to over 20,000 sales from one trade show and their approach to getting traction at each event.

**Offline Events (Chapter 22)**
Sponsoring or running offline events – from small meetups to large conferences – can be a primary way you get traction. We spoke with Rob Walling, founder and organizer of MicroConf, to talk about how to run a fantastic event, how it can benefit you, and the type of work that goes into pulling off a successful event.

**Speaking Engagements (Chapter 23)**
Eric Ries, author of the bestselling book *The Lean Startup,* told us how he used speaking engagements to hit the bestseller list within a week of the book's launch, how he landed these talks, and why he chose to use this channel to generate awareness and book sales. We also interviewed Dan Martell, founder of Clarity, to learn how to leverage a speaking event, give an awesome talk and grow your startup's profile at such speaking gigs.

**Community Building (Chapter 24)**
Companies like Zappos, Wikipedia, and Stack Exchange have all grown by forming passionate communities around their products. In our interview with Jimmy Wales of Wikipedia, he detailed how he built the Wikipedia community that's created the largest repository of human knowledge in history.

We also spoke with others who've built and scaled communities at different stages: Jeff Atwood, co-founder of Stack Exchange and Discourse; Chris McCann, founder of the popular Startup Digest newsletter; and Sandi MacPherson, founder of the community-based startup Quibb.

## *Takeaways*

- Every one of the nineteen traction channels has proven an effective means to get initial traction for both enterprise and consumer companies.

- It is hard to predict exactly which traction channel will be best for your company at a particular time.

- You have natural tendencies (bias) toward or against certain traction channels. Which traction channels are you biased for? Which traction channels are you biased against?

See our introductory resources and discuss this chapter with us and other founders on our forum:

http://tbook.us/intro

# CHAPTER 2

# The Bullseye Framework

With so many channels to consider, figuring out which one to focus on is tough. That's why we've created a simple framework called Bullseye that will help you **find the channel that will get you traction**. As billionaire PayPal founder and early Facebook investor Peter Thiel put it:

*"[You] probably won't have a bunch of equally good distribution strategies. Engineers frequently fall victim to this because they do not understand distribution. Since they don't know what works, and haven't thought about it, they try some sales, BD, advertising, and viral marketing—everything but the kitchen sink.*

*That is a really bad idea. It is very likely that one channel is optimal. Most businesses actually get zero distribution channels to work. Poor distribution—not product—is the number one cause of failure. If you can get even a single distribution channel to work, you have great business. If you try for several but don't nail one, you're finished.*

*So it's worth thinking really hard about finding the single best distribution channel."*

We use a Bullseye metaphor in our framework because you're aiming for the Bullseye—the one traction channel that will unlock your next growth stage. Using Bullseye to find your channel is a five-step process: brainstorm, rank, prioritize, test, and focus on what works. Rinse, repeat.

## *Step 1: Brainstorm*

The goal in brainstorming is to come up with reasonable ways you might use **each traction channel**. If you were to advertise offline, where would be the best place to do it? If you were to give a speech, who would be the ideal audience?

As mentioned in chapter 1, everyone approaches traction channels with biases. This first step is meant to help you systematically counteract your channel biases. That is, it is important that you **not dismiss any traction channel in this step**. You should be able to think of at least one idea for every channel – that's brainstorming!

In terms of research to feed your brainstorm, this book is a good start, but you should get much more specific to your company. You should know what marketing strategies have worked in your industry, as well as the history of companies in your space. It's especially important to understand how similar companies acquired customers over time, and how unsuccessful companies wasted their marketing dollars.

An easy way to organize your brainstorm is with a spreadsheet. We have an example one in the resources you can use as a starting point. Each column contains an idea of how you might use a particular channel. You can have many ideas per channel.

Some other suggested columns to help round out your thinking:

- How probable does it seem that this idea could work (1–5)?

- What is the expected cost to acquire a customer through this idea?

- How many customers can you expect to acquire at that cost (before saturation)?

- What is the timeframe needed to run tests?

Of course you won't know the right answers to all these questions, but you can make educated guesses.

## Step 2: Rank

The ranking step helps you organize your brainstorming efforts. It also helps you start to think a bit more critically about the traction channels in aggregate.

Place each of the traction channels into one of three columns, with each column representing a concentric circle in the Bullseye:

- Column A (Inner Circle): which traction channels seem most promising right now?

- Column B (Potential): which traction channels seem like they could possibly work?

- Column C (Long-shot): which traction channels seem like long-shots?

See the resources for a downloadable copy. Here's one example:

| Inner Circle (A) | Promising (B) | Long-shot (C) |
|---|---|---|
|  |  |  |
|  |  |  |
|  |  |  |
|  |  |  |
|  |  |  |
|  |  |  |
|  |  |  |
|  |  |  |
|  |  |  |
|  |  |  |
|  |  |  |
|  |  |  |
|  |  |  |
|  |  |  |

The research you did and ideas you came up with in the brainstorm step should guide your rankings. Usually, a few ideas you thought of will seem particularly compelling – these traction channels belong in column A. Channels with ideas that seem like they could plausibly work go in column B. Channels with only ideas that seem like more of a stretch would belong in column C.

## Step 3: Prioritize

Now identify your inner circle: the three traction channels that seem most promising. If you already have three channels in Column A, you're done! If you have more than three, then you need to get rid of some and visa-versa.

It is often the case that there are a few truly exciting and promising channels that emerge from ranking, but not a lot. Draw the line where there is an obvious drop-off in excitement. That drop-off often occurs around the third channel.

We want you to have more than one channel in your inner circle because we don't want you to waste valuable time finding your successful traction channel by testing channels sequentially when you can do so equally well in parallel.

You can run multiple experiments at the same time since tests take some time to run after they've been set up. Yet doing too many things in parallel leads to errors from lack of focus, which means the number needs to be somewhat low.

## Step 4: Test

The testing step is where you put your ideas into the real world. The goal of this step is to find out which of the traction channels in your inner circle is worth focusing on.

You will make that decision based on results from a series of relatively cheap tests. These tests should be designed to answer the following questions.

- Roughly how much will it cost to acquire customers through this channel?

- How many customers do you think are available through this channel?

- Are the customers that you are getting through this channel the ones that you want right now?

These questions are very similar to the columns we suggested making in the brainstorm step. When testing, you are replacing your educated guesses with real answers.

There isn't a single method for testing each traction channel because every business is different. We will cover tactics for organizing and thinking about these tests in chapter 4. You should also get specific ideas for each traction channel throughout the rest of the book.

Keep in mind that, when testing, **you are not trying to get a lot of traction with a channel just yet.** Instead, you are simply trying to determine if it's a channel that *could* work for your startup. Your main consideration at this point is speed to get data and prove out your assumptions.

You want to design smaller scale tests that don't require much up-front cost or effort. For example, run four Facebook ads vs. forty. You should be able to get a rough idea of a channel's effectiveness with just a few hundred dollars.

## Step 5: Focusing

If all goes well, one of the traction channels you tested in your inner circle produced promising results. In that case, you should start directing your traction efforts and resources towards that most promising channel.

**At any stage in a startup's lifecycle, one traction channel dominates in terms of customer acquisition.** That is why we suggest focusing on one at a time, and only after you've identified a channel that seems like it could actually work.

The goal of this focusing step is quite simple: to wring every bit of traction out of the traction channel. To do so, you will be continually experimenting to find out exactly how to optimize growth in your chosen channel. As you dive deeper into it, you will uncover effective tactics and do everything you can to scale them until they are no longer effective due to saturation or rising costs.

## Repeating the Process

If, unfortunately, no channel seems promising after testing, the whole process should be repeated. The good news is you now have data from all the tests you just did, which will inform you as to what types of things are, and are not, resonating with customers. Look at the messaging you've been using, or dig deeper to see at what point each channel failed to deliver customers.

## Why Use the Bullseye Framework?

Bullseye is designed to be a straightforward way to direct your traction focus and maximize your results. First and foremost, it forces you to take all the traction channels more seriously than you would otherwise. This is accomplished via the brainstorm step and then again by forcing you to think about all of the channels through the rank and prioritize steps. These steps **systematically uncover strategies for getting traction that you wouldn't have found using other approaches**.

The framework is also meant to help you zoom in on the best ideas as quickly and cheaply as possible, while still casting a wide net: hence the Bullseye metaphor.

Third, we emphasize doing tests in parallel since the traction channel that will ultimately succeed is unpredictable, and time is of the essence.

## Bullseye in the Wild

Noah Kagan talked to us about how he used a version of Bullseye at Mint, a site that helps you track your finances and was acquired by Intuit for $170 million. Their initial traction goal was 100,000 users in the first six months after launch.

In steps 1–3, Noah and his team brainstormed and picked several traction channels that seemed promising (targeting blogs, pr, search engine marketing) – their inner circle.

In step 4, they then ran a series of cheap tests in each (sponsored a small newsletter, reached out to financial celebrities like Suze Orman, placed some Google ads) to see what worked and what didn't. Noah kept track of the test results in this spreadsheet:

| Source | Traffic | CTR | Conversion % | Total Users | Status | Confirmed | Confirmed Users |
|---|---|---|---|---|---|---|---|
| TechCrunch | 300000 | 10% | 25% | 7500 | Friend | Yes | 7500 |
| Dave McClure | 30000 | 10% | 25% | 750 | Friend | Yes | 750 |
| Mashable | 500000 | 10% | 25% | 12500 | Emailing | No | 0 |
| Reddit | 25000 | 100% | 25% | 6250 | Coordinated | Yes | 6250 |
| Digg | 100000 | 100% | 25% | 25000 | Coordinated | Yes | 25000 |
| Google Organic | 5000 | 100% | 15% | 750 | Receiving | Yes | 750 |
| Google Ads | 1000000 | 3% | 35% | 10500 | Bought | Yes | 10500 |
| Paul Stamatiou | 50000 | 5% | 50% | 1250 | Friend | Yes | 1250 |
| Personal Finance Sponsorships | 200000 | 40% | 65% | 52000 | Coordinated | Yes | 52000 |
| Okdork.com | 3000 | 10% | 75% | 225 | Self | Yes | 225 |
| | | | | | | | |
| Total Users | | | | 116725 | | | 104225 |

Step 5: after running these experiments, Mint focused on the traction channel that seemed most promising and that could reach their goal. In this case, that meant targeting blogs. In the early days, the tactics of sponsoring mid-level bloggers in the financial niche and guest posting allowed them to acquire their first 40,000 customers.

When this channel maxed out, they repeated the Bullseye process, and found a new traction channel to focus on: public relations. Within 6 months of launching, they had 1 million users. We cover specific strategies for both these traction channels in later chapters.

We heard stories like this over and over again when talking to successful startup founders. They would research many channels, try a few, and focus on the most promising until it stopped working. Bullseye is designed to systemize this successful process. Use it!

## Takeaways

- The Bullseye Framework is a five-step repeatable process to maximize your chances of getting traction: brainstorm, rank, prioritize, test, and focus.

- Focusing on a traction channel means becoming an expert on it by continually testing new tactics to get the most traction possible.

- Research how past and present companies in your space and adjacent spaces succeeded or failed at getting traction. The easiest way to do this is to go talk to startup founders who previously failed at what you're trying to do.

- Compile your brainstorming ideas for each traction channel in a spreadsheet with educated guesses that you can confirm through testing.

See our introductory resources and discuss this chapter with us and other startup founders on our forum:

http://tbook.us/bullseye

# CHAPTER 3

# Traction Thinking

Bullseye helps you determine which traction channels to focus on at any given time, but doesn't give you any specific strategies or tactics for how to focus on traction channels. That's what the rest of this book is for. This chapter presents traction strategies you should employ across each traction channel.

## *The 50% Rule*

If you're starting a company, chances are you can build a product. **Almost every failed startup has a product. What failed startups don't have are enough customers.**

Marc Andreessen, founder of Netscape and VC firm Andreessen-Horowitz, sums up this common problem:

*"The number one reason that we pass on entrepreneurs we'd otherwise like to back is their focusing on product to the exclusion of everything else. Many entrepreneurs who build great products simply don't have a good distribution strategy. Even worse is when they insist that they don't need one, or call [their] no distribution strategy a 'viral marketing strategy.'"*

A common story goes like this: founders build something people want by following a sound product development strategy. They spend their time building new features based on what early users say they want.

Then, when they think they are ready, they launch, take stabs at getting more users, only to become frustrated when customers don't flock to them.

Having a product your early customers love but no clear way to get more traction is frustrating. To address this frustration, spend your time building product **and testing traction channels – in parallel.**

Building something people want is required for traction, but isn't enough. There are many situations where you could build something people want, but still not end up with a viable business.

Some examples: you build something users want but can't figure out a useful business model – users won't pay, won't click on adverts, etc. (no market). You build something people want, but there are just not enough users to reach profitability (small market). You build something users want, but reaching them is cost prohibitive (hard to reach market). Finally, you build something users want, but a lot of other companies build it too, and so it is too hard to get customers (competitive market).

In other words, traction and product development are of equal importance and should **each get about half of your attention. This is what we call the 50% rule: spend 50% of your time on product and 50% on traction.** This split is hard to do because the pull to spend all of your attention on product is strong, and splitting your time will certainly slow down product development. However, it won't slow the time to get your product successfully to market. That's because pursuing product development and traction in parallel has several key benefits.

First, it helps you build a better product because you can incorporate knowledge from your traction efforts. If you're following a good product development process, you're already getting good feedback from early users. Traction development gets you additional data, like what messaging is resonating with potential users, what niche you might focus on first, what types of customers will be easiest to acquire, and major distribution roadblocks you might run into.

You will get some of this information through good product development practices, but not nearly enough. All of this new information should change the first version of the product for the better.

This is exactly what happened with Dropbox. While developing their product, they tested search engine marketing and found it wouldn't work for their business. They were acquiring customers for $230 when their product only cost $99. That's when they focused on the viral marketing channel, and built a referral program right into their product. This program has since been their biggest growth driver.

In contrast, waiting until you ship a product to embark on traction development usually results in one or more additional product development cycles as you adjust to real market feedback. That's why doing traction and product development in parallel may slow down product development in the short run, but not in the long run.

The second benefit to parallel product and traction development is that you get to experiment and test different traction channels before you launch anything. This means when your product is ready, you can grow rapidly. A head start on understanding the traction channel that will work for your business is invaluable. Phil Fernandez, founder and CEO of Marketo, a marketing automation company that IPO'ed in 2013, talks about this benefit:

*"At Marketo, not only did we have SEO [Search Engine Optimization] in place even before product development, we also had a blog. We talked about the problems we aimed to solve... Instead of beta testing a product, we beta tested an idea and integrated the feedback we received from our readers early on in our product development process.*

*By using this content strategy, we at Marketo began drumming up interest in our solutions with so much advance notice we had a pipeline of more than 14,000 interested buyers when the product came to market."*

Marketo wouldn't have had 14,000 interested buyers if they just focused on product development.

It's the difference between significant customer growth on day one – real traction – and just a product you know some people want.

## Comparison to Lean

Many good product development methodologies exist, but don't deal explicitly with getting traction. The Lean Startup framework is a popular one. This approach involves creating testable hypotheses regarding your product, and then going out and validating (or invalidating) those hypotheses. It's an approach that demands a great deal of interaction with customers, discovering their needs and understanding the types of features they require.

Bullseye works hand-in-hand with Lean. What Lean is to product development, Bullseye is to traction. With Lean, you figure out the right features to build. With Bullseye, you figure out the right traction channel to pursue.

To reiterate, **the biggest mistake startups make when trying to get traction is failing to pursue traction in parallel with product development.**

Many entrepreneurs think that if you build a killer product, your customers will beat a path to your door. We call this line of thinking The Product Trap: the fallacy that the best use of your time is always improving your product. In other words, "if you build it, they will come" is wrong.

You are much more likely to develop a good distribution strategy with a good traction development methodology (like Bullseye) the same way you are much more likely to develop a good product with a good product development methodology (like Lean). Both help address major risks that face early stage companies: market risk (that you can reach customers in a sustainable way) and product risk (that customers want what you're building), respectively.

Pursuing both traction and product in parallel will increase your chances of success by both developing a product for which you can actually get traction and getting traction with that product much sooner.

## Moving the Needle

Your traction strategy should always be focused on moving the needle for your company. By moving the needle, we mean focusing on marketing activities that **result in a measurable, significant impact on your company**. It should be something that advances your user acquisition goals in a meaningful way, not something that would be just a blip even if it worked.

For example, early on DuckDuckGo focused on search engine optimization to get in front of users searching for "new search engine." In the early days, these users really moved the needle and were the biggest source of growth. Eventually, DuckDuckGo's userbase outstripped this volume by many times, and they had to move onto another traction channel that moved the needle.

From the perspective of getting traction, you can think about working on a product in three phases:

Phase I – making something people want

Phase II – marketing something people want

Phase III – scaling your business

Phase I is very product focused and involves pursuing initial traction while also building your initial product as we discussed above. This often means getting traction in ways that don't scale – giving talks, writing guest posts, emailing people you have relationships with, attending conferences and doing whatever you can to get in front of customers.

As Paul Graham said in his essay "Do Things that Don't Scale:"

*"One of the most common types of advice we give at Y Combinator is to do things that don't scale. A lot of would-be founders believe that startups either take off or don't. You build something, make it available, and if you've made a better mousetrap, people beat a path to your door as promised. Or they don't, in which case the market must not exist.*

*Actually startups take off because the founders make them take off... The most common unscalable thing founders have to do at the start is to recruit users manually. Nearly all startups have to. You can't wait for users to come to you. You have to go out and get them."*

If you've made it to phase II, you have a product that resonates with customers – initial traction – and therefore doesn't require sweeping product changes. In other words, in phase II you have established product/market fit and now are fine-tuning your positioning and marketing messages.

In phase III, you have an established business model, significant position in the market, and are focused on scaling both to further dominate the market and to profit.

At different product phases, moving the needle means different things. In phase I, it's getting those first few customers. In phase II, it is getting enough customers where you're knocking on the door of sustainability. And, in phase III, your focus is on increasing your earnings, scaling your marketing channels, and creating a truly sustainable business.

Some traction channels will move the needle early on, but will fail to work later. Others are hard to get working in phase I, but are major sources of traction in the later phases (PR is a good example). On the other hand, some channels will be great in phase I but useless in phases II and III because they simply don't have the volume required to move the needle.

When you're just starting out, small things can move the needle in terms of traction. A single tweet from a well-respected individual or a speech to a few hundred people at a meetup can result in a meaningful jump in users.

As your company grows, smaller things like that will be difficult to notice. If you have 10,000 visitors to your website each day, it will be hard to appreciate a tweet or blog post that sends 200 visitors your way. As your startup sees more traction, things that worked early on may not scale well (or be worth scaling). What moves the needle changes dramatically.

Moving the needle in the later stages requires larger and larger numbers. If you want to add 100,000 new customers, with conversion rates between 1–5%, you're looking at reaching 2–10 million people – those are huge numbers! That's why traction channels like community building and viral marketing can be so powerful: they scale with the size of your userbase and potential market.

Startup growth happens in spurts. Initially, growth is usually slow. Then, it spikes as a useful traction channel is unlocked. Eventually it flattens out again as a channel gets saturated and becomes less effective. Then, you unlock another strategy and you get another spike. That's why the cover of our book looks the way it does.

In other words, the way you get traction will change. **After your growth curve flattens, what worked before usually will not get you to the next level**. On the flip side, traction channels that seemed like long shots before might be worth reconsidering during your next iteration of Bullseye.

You can think of your initial investment in traction as pouring water into a leaky bucket. In phase I, your bucket will be leaky because your product is not yet a full solution to customer needs and problems. In other words, your product is not as sticky as it could be and many customers will not want to engage with it yet. As a consequence, much of the money you are spending on traction will leak out of your bucket.

There is no reason to scale up your efforts now. You are throwing much of your money away!

As you hone your product, you are effectively plugging leaks. Once you have crossed over to phase II, you have product-market fit and customers are sticking around. Now is time to scale up your traction efforts: your bucket is no longer leaky.

When you constantly test traction channels by sending through a steady stream of new users, you can tell how leaky your bucket is. You can also tell if it is getting less leaky over time, which it should be if your product development strategy is sound. In fact this is a great feedback loop between traction development and product development that you can use to make sure you're on the right track.

## How Much Traction Is Enough for Investors?

Startup founders tend to focus on fundraising, often out of necessity. As a result, they often wonder how much traction they need to get investors interested. Naval Ravikant, founder of AngelList answers this question well:

*"It is a moving target. The entire ecosystem is getting far more efficient. Companies are accomplishing a lot more with a lot less.*

*Two years ago (Nov 2010) you could have gotten your daily deal startup funded pre-traction. Eighteen months ago you could not have gotten a daily deal startup funded no matter how much traction you had. Twelve months ago you could have gotten your mobile app company funded with ten thousand downloads. Today it's probably going to take a few hundred thousand downloads and a strong rapid adoption rate for a real financing to take place.*

*The definition of traction keeps changing as the environment gets competitive. That's why it is actually useful to look at AngelList and look at companies just got funded; that will give you an idea of where the bar is right now."*

It is also a good idea to first reach out to individuals who intimately understand what you're working on (perhaps since they have worked on or invested in something similar before).

**The better your prospective investors understand what you're doing, the less traction they will need to see before they invest** because they are more likely to extrapolate your little traction and believe it could grow into something big. On the other hand, those investors that have little real-world experience within your industry may find it hard to extrapolate and may demand more traction initially before they invest. An outlier is friends and family, who may not need to see any traction before investing since they're investing in you personally.

You may not have the benefit of reaching out to people who are familiar with you or your work. In this case, you will want to do your homework on prospective investors. Again, the ones most likely to understand your company (because they've made similar investments or have done similar companies before) are the ones you should approach first.

It is easy to get discouraged when you are fundraising because you can get so many rejections. However, you shouldn't take rejection as a rejection of your idea. **There are many reasons why investors may say no that are simply beyond your control (investment goals, timing, expertise, etc.).**

Remember that different investors have different goals. Some are looking for home runs and so are focused on turning a big profit. Others are looking for a single or a double, and will therefore be more looking at your revenue and current traction strategy. Others still are simply looking to get involved with something interesting.

Likewise, some investors may focus on revenue and profitability while others may want to see evidence of intense product engagement.

Product engagement means different things for different startups, but generally it means real customers using your product because it is solving some problem or need for them. **Sustainable product engagement growth (i.e. more customers getting engaged over time) is hard for any investor to ignore.**

This is true even if your absolute numbers are relatively small. So if you only have 100 customers, but have been growing 10% a month for six months, that's attractive to investors. With sustainable growth, you look like a good bet to succeed in the long run.

## To Pivot or Not to Pivot

You may come to a point where you are simply unhappy with your traction. You may not be able to raise funding or just feel like things aren't taking off the way they should. How do you know when to "pivot" from what you're doing?

We strongly believe that many startups give up way too early. **A lot of startup success hinges on choosing a great market at the right time.** Consider DuckDuckGo, the search engine startup that Gabriel founded. Other search startups gave up after two years: Gabriel has been at it for more than six.

Privacy has been a core differentiator for DuckDuckGo (they do not track you) since 2009 but didn't become a mainstream issue until the NSA leaks in 2013. Growth was steady before 2013, but exploded as privacy became something everyone was talking about.

It's important to wrap your head around this time-scale. If you are just starting out, are you ready to potentially do this for the *next decade*? In retrospect, a lot of founders feel they picked their company idea too quickly, and they would have picked something they were more passionate about if they realized it was such a long haul. A startup can be awesome if you believe in it: if not, it can get old quickly.

**If you are considering a pivot, the first thing to look for is evidence of real product engagement**, even if it is only a few dedicated customers. If you have such engagement, you might be giving up too soon. You should examine these bright spots to see how they might be expanded. Why do these customers take to your product so well? Is there some thread that unites them? Are they early adopters in a huge market or are they outliers? The answers to these questions may reveal some promise that is not immediately evident in your core metrics.

Another factor to consider before you pivot: startup founders are usually forward thinking and as a result are often too early to markets (that's why it's important to choose a startup idea you're willing to stick with for many years). Granted, there is a big difference between being a few years too early and a decade too early. Hardly anyone can stick around for ten years with middling results. But, being a year or two early can be a great thing. You can use this time to improve and refine your product. Then, when the market takes off, you have a head start on competitors just entering your space.

How can you tell whether you are just a bit early to market and should keep plugging away? Again, the best way to find out is by looking for evidence of product engagement. If you are a little early to a market there should be some early adopters out there already eating up what you have to offer.

## Takeaways

- Don't fall into The Product Trap: pursue traction and product development in parallel, and spend equal time on both.

- The Bullseye Framework and a product development framework (e.g. Lean Startup) can work together to maximize your probability of success.

- Focus on strategies and tactics that can plausibly move the needle for company. What change in growth metrics would move the needle for your company?

- How much traction is needed for investors is a moving target, but a sustainable customer growth rate is hard for investors to ignore. Potential investors who understand your business are likely to appreciate your traction and thus invest earlier.

- If you're not seeing the traction you want, look for bright spots in your userbase, pockets of users that are truly engaged with your product. See if you can figure out why it works for them and if you can expand from that base. If there are no bright spots, it may be a good time to pivot.

See our introductory resources and discuss this chapter with us and other startup founders on our forum:

http://tbook.us/intro

# CHAPTER 4

# Traction Testing

Continuous testing is the key to getting traction with Bullseye. When searching for a traction channel to focus on, you're testing the channels in your inner circle to see which are most promising. Then, when you find one worth your undivided attention, you test tactics within that channel to wring the most traction from it. In this chapter, we cover how to approach testing.

## *The Law of Shitty Click-Throughs*

Andrew Chen, a startup advisor on growth, coined the Law of Shitty Click-Throughs: *"Over time, all marketing strategies result in shitty click-through rates."* (Click-through rate refers to the response rate of a marketing campaign.)

What this means is that over time, all marketing channels become saturated. As more companies discover an effective strategy, it becomes crowded and expensive or ignored by consumers, thus becoming much less effective. When banner ads first debuted, they were receiving click-through rates of over 75%! Once they became commonplace, click-through rates plummeted.

This happens with all channels: strategies that once worked well will become crowded and ineffective. All it takes is one other competitor seriously pursuing traction in the same channel to drive up its cost and drive down its efficacy.

To combat this reality you should consistently conduct small experiments. **Constantly running small traction tests will allow you to stay ahead of competitors pursuing the same channels.** As Andrew puts it:

*"The ... solution to solving the Law of Shitty Click-Throughs, even momentarily, is to discover the next untapped marketing [strategy]... If you can make these [strategy] work with a strong product behind it, then great. Chances are, you'll enjoy a few months if not a few years of strong marketing performance before they too slowly succumb."*

Consistently running cheap tests will also allow you to discover new techniques with amazing results. For example, you might be able to take advantage of new marketing platforms while they are still in their infancy. Zynga did this with Facebook, dominating their advertising and sharing features when there was relatively little competition. For a gaming company today, it's basically impossible to leverage Facebook to grow the way Zynga did just a few years ago – it's just too expensive and too crowded.

## Inner Circle Tests

When trying to figure out what traction channel to focus on using Bullseye, you run cheap tests on the traction channels in your inner circle. The goal of these tests is to validate or invalidate assumptions you have about strategies in these traction channels. For example:

- How much does it cost to acquire customers through this channel strategy?

- How many customers are available through this channel strategy?

- How well do these customers convert?

- How long does it take to acquire a customer?

These are the assumptions to plug into your model (usually a spreadsheet) that will determine which channel and strategies to focus on.

For example, for targeting blogs you might have questions about which blogs, what type of content, etc. For search engine marketing, the questions would be more about keywords, ad copy, and landing pages, whereas with social ads they would be more about target demographics, ad copy and landing pages. Each traction channel has slightly different questions to answer.

Once you know your assumptions, devise specific tests to validate them as cheaply as possible. **These first tests in a channel are often very cheap**: for instance, if you spend just $250 on AdWords, you'll get a rough idea of how well the search engine marketing channel works for your business.

With limited resources, it's almost impossible to optimize multiple strategies at once. Running ten social ads and testing everything about them (ad copy, landing pages, etc.) is a full-time endeavor. *That is optimization, not testing.* Rather, you should be running several cheap tests (perhaps two social ads with two landing pages) that give some indication of how successful a given channel or channel strategy could be.

Really focusing on a channel takes significant time and resources. This time is valuable and should only be used after you have some indication that a given traction channel or strategy within it will likely work. Sean Ellis, growth advisor to Dropbox and Eventbrite, had this to say about this approach:

*"The faster you run high quality experiments, the more likely you'll find scalable, effective growth tactics. Determining the success of a customer acquisition idea is dependent on an effective tracking and reporting system, so don't start testing until your tracking/reporting system has been implemented."*

This "effective tracking and reporting system" can be as complex as an analytics tool that does cohort analysis or can be as simple as a spreadsheet, but it must exist. Furthermore, each cheap test you run should have a point – to validate or invalidate specific assumption(s) in your model.

## Optimization Through A/B Testing

After you've run cheap tests, validated assumptions, and found a traction channel that is working, your goal is optimize your use of that channel. A/B testing (also known as split testing) is a tactic that helps you do just that.

In its most basic form, A/B testing is a science experiment with a control group (A) and an experimental group (B). A/B testing is often called split testing because for the best results you split people (randomly) into one of the two groups, and then measure what they do.

The purpose of an A/B test is to measure the effectiveness of a change in one or more variables – for example, a button color, an ad image, or a different message on one of your web pages. You create one version of your page for your control group and a second version for your experimental group. As you track how each page performs, you can find out whether your changes are having an impact on a key metric like signups. If, after a period of time, the experimental group performs significantly better, you can apply the change, reap the benefits and run another test.

**Making A/B testing a habit (even if you just run 1 test a week) will improve your efficiency in a traction channel by 2–3x.** There are many tools to help you do this type of testing, such as Optimizely, Visual Website Optimizer, and Unbounce. These tools allow you to test optimizations without making complex changes to your code.

## Online Tools

Every day more online tools come on the market to help you optimize traction channels. We just mentioned a few related to A/B testing. We highly recommend **embracing the use of online tools to help you understand and assess the efficacy of all your traction efforts.**

For example, the questions below seem like they are difficult or might require a lot of research to answer:

- How many prospective customers landed on my website?

- What are the demographics of my best and worst customers?

- Are customers who interact with my support team more likely to stay customers longer?

However, they are quite straightforward if you're using the right online tools. In fact, a basic analytics tool like Clicky, Google Analytics or Mixpanel can help you answer all three of these questions. These tools tell you who is coming to your site, at what frequency, and, perhaps most importantly, when and where they are leaving your site.

In the online resources for this chapter we point you to a variety of relevant analytics tools. In later chapters we recommend tools for specific traction channels.

## Quantify Your Results

The Bullseye Framework we outlined in chapter 2 didn't explicitly involve a lot of numbers. We wanted to make it accessible. But when we apply our framework, we make it a bit more quantitative. The reason for doing so is simple – **there are some quantitative metrics that are universal across traction channels.**

We recommend using a spreadsheet to help you rank and prioritize your traction channels.

At a minimum, include the columns of *cost to acquire a customer* and *lifetime value of a customer* within a given traction channel. Since these metrics are universal, you can use them to easily make comparisons across channels. In general, we encourage you to be as quantitative as possible, even if it is initially just guesstimating.

As we mentioned in chapter 3, you should only be thinking about traction channels and specific strategies that have a chance of moving the needle for your startup. You can assess what can move the needle with some simple calculations. For example, how many customers do you think a given traction channel strategy could deliver? How many new customers do you need to really move the needle?

If there is no reasonable chance this channel strategy could yield enough new customers to move the needle within your current budget, then it is probably not worth exploring. For example, focusing on getting articles on tech news sites doesn't make sense right now for DuckDuckGo because they couldn't possibly convert enough people to make a significant difference in the company's search numbers. However, this strategy did work in phase I.

Quantifying the number of users you might add becomes even more important in phase II and phase III when you already have product-market fit. In that case most channels will give you some users, and so they are all tempting to some degree. The operative question then is, "Does this channel have enough users to be meaningful?" A back-of-the-envelope calculation can go a long way!

## Takeaways

- Keep a look out for the cutting edge tactics that haven't yet succumbed to the Law of Shitty Click-Throughs.

- Run cheap tests to validate quantitative assumptions from a model (e.g. a spreadsheet).

- You should consistently run A/B tests in your efforts to optimize a traction channel. There are many online tools that can help you test easier and evaluate your use of various traction channels.

- Look for ways to quantify your marketing efforts, especially when deciding what traction strategies to pursue and comparing traction channels within Bullseye. You should have an idea at all times of what numbers it will take to move the needle, and focus your traction efforts only on strategies that could possibly do so.

See our introductory resources and discuss this chapter with us and other startup founders on our forum:

http://tbook.us/intro

# CHAPTER 5

# Critical Path

Startups get pulled in a lot of different directions. There are always opportunities in front of you or on the horizon that you could focus on. There are always product revisions you could work on. There are always background tasks nagging at you. How do you decide what to work on?

## Defining your Critical Path

Let's assume you buy into our approach to getting traction. You're following the 50% rule and spending half your time pursuing traction. You've followed Bullseye and have a promising traction channel to focus on.

As we said in the introduction, *traction trumps everything*. Because of that, what you choose to focus on should relate directly back to traction.

## Your Traction Goal

**You should always have a traction goal you're working towards.** This could be 1,000 paying customers, 100 new daily users, or 10% of your market.

The right goal is highly dependent on your business. It should be chosen carefully and align with your company strategy. If you reach this goal, what will change significantly? Perhaps you'd be profitable, be able to raise money more easily, or become the market leader.

At DuckDuckGo the current traction goal is one percent of the general search market. Achieving that goal is meaningful because at that point they will be taken much more seriously as an entrenched part of the market and everything that comes with that recognition (better deals, PR, etc.).

This traction goal wouldn't work well for most other companies because usually one percent of a well-defined market is not that significant or valuable. It works in the general search engine space because the market is so big and there are so few companies in it. This speaks to the importance of setting a traction goal that is particularly significant for your company.

Before this traction goal, DuckDuckGo had a traction goal of 100 million searches a month, which took them to about a break-even point. Getting to break-even was the company significance that was aligned with that traction goal.

Before that the goal was to get the product and messaging to a point where people were switching to DuckDuckGo as their primary search engine and sticking indefinitely. The company significance there was to move from phase I to II and get true product/market fit.

These are big goals. In DuckDuckGo's case their traction goals have each taken about two years to achieve. The timescale is not important, however. The significance to your company is important. If the significance you are trying to achieve is profitability and you think you can get there in six months then that's great!

## Defining Milestones

**The path to reaching your traction goal with the fewest number of steps is your Critical Path.** It helps to literally draw this path out, enumerating the intermediate steps (milestones) to get to your traction goal. These milestones need not be traction related, but should be ***absolutely necessary* to reach your goal.**

In DuckDuckGo's case, their traction goal was to get to 100 million searches/month. They believed milestones they needed to hit included a faster site, a more compelling mobile offering and more broadcast TV coverage (in the PR traction channel).

Even though product features like images and auto-suggest were continually requested, they believed they were not absolutely necessary milestones in their Critical Path to reach that traction goal. However, now that they are on the traction goal to get to one percent of the search market, these product features are believed to now be necessary milestones on this new Critical Path.

The reasoning for why these particular features weren't necessary initially was that even at 100 million/searches month their userbase was motivated enough by other features to be forgiving of missing these particular ones. However, to get to the next traction goal they had to get more mainstream adoption and this next set of users is much less forgiving.

In your company, your milestones will be different, but the point is to be critical and strategic in deciding what to include. That's why it is called the Critical Path. For example, you may think to reach your traction goal you will need to hire three people, add features A, B and C to your product, and engage in marketing activities X, Y, and Z. These are *the milestones* you need to do to get where you want to go.

Next, order your milestones by which need to be done first, second and so forth. For example, in Bullseye you want to run small tests to validate assumptions about a traction channel before focusing on it. DuckDuckGo set out to get on broadcast TV once and confirm that strategy could move the needle before focusing on it.

In your product, you may need to build feature A before B because B depends on A. In other words, you're identifying dependencies. You should also strive to figure out the shortest path. DuckDuckGo often first incorporates software from external providers before embarking on a more complicated build-out themselves.

The order of your absolutely necessary milestones is your Critical Path. Once you've defined your critical path, it's easy to determine the direction to go in – just follow the path! In particular, work on the first step(s) and **nothing else**. After these first steps are complete, re-assess your critical path using the market knowledge you just learned from achieving that milestone.

Your original plan is often wrong. For example, you thought you had to build features A, B, C to get to your traction goal, but after building A and getting market feedback you realize you need to skip B and build C and D. That's why a hard re-assessment after each step is necessary.

This method helps you decide what *not* to do. **Everything you do should be assessed against your Critical Path.** Every activity is either on path or not. If it is not on the path, don't do it!

## Employee and Department Critical Paths

We've been talking so far about your whole company's Critical Path. Pieces of your company have their own critical paths, from departments (marketing, engineering) down to individual people. The sum of these paths is your company's Critical Path.

It's important to continually define these sub-critical paths down to the individual level for the same reason as it is important to define the whole company Critical Path. Doing so forces your people to work towards the right goals in the most efficient way possible.

At DuckDuckGo recall the current traction goal is one percent of the search market. They're at about half that now and are doing things in each department that could move the needle towards that number. For example, the engineering critical path is to get out features that they

know are holding mainstream people back from sticking on the search engine (images, autosuggest).

Going even lower, the iOS teams' critical path is to put out an update for iOS 7 to bring that experience more in-line with desktop. And deeper still an individual critical path on that team is to finalize the designs for that product refresh.

Similarly with regards to traction and Bullseye, departments can have their own traction goals and milestones. Sticking with the DuckDuckGo mobile example, they had a traction goal one million app users and decided after running tests through Bullseye that getting featured in the iOS app store was the next marketing strategy milestone. At that point, they promptly stopped activity on trying to get press, run ads and many other app traction strategies because they were no longer on path.

Management at all levels constantly works to refine the Critical Path based on market feedback. At DuckDuckGo everyone has weekly 1–1s and company-wide meetings with a standing agenda item to corroborate the current paths. Usually this is very brief since they don't change that much on a weekly basis. After a milestone is achieved, however, longer strategic discussions take place. Having time already carved out for these discussions ensures they happen in a timely fashion and that they get taken seriously enough to change individual, department and company direction.

## Defining Traction Sub-goals

The importance of choosing the right traction goal cannot be overstated. Are you going for growth or profitability, or something in between? If you need to raise money in X months, what traction do you need to show to do so? These are the types of questions that help you determine the right traction goal.

Once defined, you can work backwards and set clear quantitative and time-based traction sub-goals, like reaching 1,000 customers by next quarter or hitting 20% monthly growth.

Doing so allows you to benchmark your traction progress and see definitively what's working and what's not. It also makes it easier to evaluate what will move the needle for a given timeframe, since you have a concrete goal for how much the needle has to move.

Another benefit of setting clear sub-goals is the accountability it provides. By placing traction activities on the same calendar as product development and other company milestones, you ensure that enough of your time will be spent on traction.

Critical Path is a high-level framework that helps you decide where to allocate your time and energy to get traction faster. Your traction goal dictates your company direction. That's because building product, getting funding and everything else your company does is in the pursuit of traction. Remember, *traction trumps everything*.

## Get Good Mentors

Without a doubt, good mentors help you stay on your critical path. Mentors are more operationally removed from your company, and so can give you a more objective perspective when you're re-assessing your traction goal. Additionally, the **simple act of preparing to meet with your mentor(s) on a regular basis is a forcing function that compels you to think more critically.**

When it comes to traction in particular, founders who have focused on similar channels or been successful in your industry can make great mentors. They're familiar with many relevant traction strategies and can give ongoing advice. Someone with this kind of experience and expertise is exceptionally valuable.

Good mentors can help you in many other areas as well. Building a company is a long, hard road fraught with traps. They can help you avoid some of those traps and make the process easier and more fun.

**Aim high.** You are a founder starting a serious, high-impact company. Anyone who is also passionate about what you're working on should be thrilled to be part of your journey.

## Overcoming Your Biases

Our Bullseye Framework helps you determine the traction milestones you need to hit, and thus set your Critical Path. It helps you find a promising traction channel to focus on, and discover successful marketing activities within that channel.

When creating this part of the Critical Path, many founders unfortunately ignore promising traction channels due to natural biases. This is an expensive proposition since it wastes resources sending you down the wrong path.

To refresh your memory, here are the nineteen channels:

1. Viral Marketing

2. Public Relations (PR)

3. Unconventional PR

4. Search Engine Marketing (SEM)

5. Social and Display Ads

6. Offline Ads

7. Search Engine Optimization (SEO)

8. Content Marketing

9. Email Marketing

10. Engineering as Marketing

11. Target Market Blogs

12. Business Development (BD)

13. Sales

14. Affiliate Programs

15. Existing Platforms

16. Trade Shows

17. Offline Events

18. Speaking Engagements

19. Community Building

We're sure that some of these channels are unfamiliar to you. Why spend time and money on a channel you know little about, or you think is irrelevant to your business?

**This bias may be preventing you from getting traction.** You can get a competitive advantage by acquiring customers in ways your competition isn't.

A major function of this book is simply helping you overcome your biases against particular traction channels. There are three reasons why founders ignore potentially profitable traction channels:

1. Out of sight, out of mind. Startups generally don't think of things like speaking engagements because they are usually out of their field of vision.

2. Some founders refuse to seriously consider channels they view negatively, like sales or affiliate marketing. Just because you hate talking on the phone doesn't mean your customers do.

3. Bias against schlep – things that seem annoying and time consuming. Channels like business development and trade shows often fall in this category.

Be honest with yourself: which traction channels are you currently biased for or against?

You can overcome your traction channel biases and increase your chances of success by taking each channel seriously when using Bullseye. Good mentors can also help you here by helping you brainstorm and rank your channel ideas. Jason Cohen, who we interviewed for offline ads, makes this point well:

*"I'll bet you a lot of your competition will refuse to even try these channels. And if that's true, that's even more reason to go try those channels! It can almost be a competitive advantage (at least a temporary one) if you can acquire customers in channels that others cannot, or refuse to try. That's more interesting than duking it out with AdWords competitors in positions 1–3."*

## How This Book Can Get You Traction

Traction is a tricky thing. Initial traction is unpredictable and can happen in many different ways – nineteen by our count. Because of this unpredictability, it makes sense to consider several channels in the pursuit of traction. In fact, **every one of the channels listed above has been *the* channel for both enterprise and consumer startups to get initial traction.**

At the same time, no one individual is an expert on all channels. However, certain people – namely startup founders who focus on them – end up becoming experts on particular channels. We set out to collect and synthesize all this knowledge from founders and other experts with deep experience in each traction channel.

The startup experts we interviewed have founded companies that have made hundreds of millions of dollars, received billion dollar valuations and built some of the biggest companies on the Internet.

With this book, we're giving you what worked for these founders and arming you with tools to help you get similar traction.

We've already covered a system to figure out which channel to focus on – Bullseye – and how to go about doing so – Critical Path. The rest of the book helps you approach getting traction through channel.

To your startup's success!

## Takeaways

- Determine your traction goal and define your Critical Path against that goal, working backwards and enumerating the company absolutely necessary milestones you need to achieve to get there.

- Stay on Critical Path by assessing every activity you do against it and by consistently re-assessing it. Building such assessment into your management processes is a good idea.

- Quantify traction sub-goals and put them on a calendar and/ or in a spreadsheet so you can properly monitor your progress over time.

- Find a good mentor or set of mentors.

- Actively work to overcome your traction channel biases. Mentors can help here.

- Being on the cutting edge of the right traction channel can make a huge difference in success. Which traction channels do you know most about? Which traction channels do you know least about?

See our introductory resources and discuss this chapter with us and other startup founders on our forum:

http://tbook.us/cpath

# CHAPTER 6

# Viral Marketing

Viral marketing is the process of getting your existing users to refer others to your product. You've seen examples of this traction channel in action any time a friend's Pinterest post appeared in your Facebook feed, or whenever you've received an email from a friend telling you about a product.

In the context of startups, going viral means that every user you acquire brings in *at least* one other user: that new user then invites another user, and so on. This creates true exponential growth. Though difficult to sustain, it's been the driving force behind the explosive growth of consumer startups like Facebook, Twitter and WhatsApp.

As great as your product may be, true viral growth is unlikely. However, this channel is so powerful that it may still be worthwhile creating referral programs where your users can refer others to your product. When these viral loops work, customers sign up in great numbers at very low acquisition cost.

We interviewed Andrew Chen, founder of Muzy (an app with more than 25 million users) and one of the experts in the viral marketing world. According to Andrew, this traction channel is becoming increasingly important as Facebook, email, and App Stores have emerged as "super-platforms" with billions of active users. As a result, companies can go viral faster than ever before. Dropbox, Instagram, and Pinterest are great examples: each leveraged virality and these super-platforms to acquire tens of millions of users in less than three years.

## Viral Loops

A viral loop in its most basic form is a three-step process:

1.  A user is exposed to your product.

2.  That user tells a set of potential users about your product.

3.  These potential users are exposed to your product and become users themselves.

The process then begins again with these new users. It's called a loop because it repeats over and over again; as your users refer other users, those users refer others, and so on.

Though viral loops share the same basic structure, each company executes them differently. Dropbox's loop is different from Pinterest's, which is different from Skype's. We're going to describe the main kinds of viral loops and show you how companies have used them to succeed.

The oldest form of virality occurs when your product is so remarkable that people naturally tell others about it – **pure word of mouth**. Word of mouth drove Facebook's early growth among college students, before they started building in more explicit viral hooks (email invites, adding your friends via address books, etc.). Word of mouth also causes many movies, books, diets and TV shows to take off.

**Inherent** virality occurs when you can only get value from a product by inviting other users.

For example, if your friends don't have Skype, the application is worthless. Apps like Snapchat and WhatsApp also fall into this category. This type of virality comes with the advantage of "network effects," where the value of the network increases as more people get on it. That is, the more people are on Skype, the more valuable it becomes.

Other products grow by encouraging **collaboration**. In this case, the product is still valuable on its own but becomes more so as you invite others. Google Docs is useful alone, but it is far more valuable when used collaboratively. This type of viral loop can take longer to spread if your users don't need to immediately collaborate, but once they do strong network effects kick-in as the service becomes a central tool around which collaboration occurs.

Another common case is to embed virality into **communications** from the product. Hotmail put a "Get a free email account with Hotmail. Sign up now." as a default signature and Apple similarly appends "sent from my iPhone." As a result, every message sent spreads the word about the product. Many software products do this with their free users. MailChimp, Weebly, UserVoice, and Desk all add branding to free customer's emails and websites by default, which can be removed by becoming a paying user.

Products can also **incentivize** their users to move through their viral loops and tell others about the product. Dropbox gives you more space if you get friends to sign up. AirBnB, Uber, PayPal and Gilt give you account credits for referring the product to friends.

Companies like reddit and YouTube have grown virally by using **embedded** buttons and widgets. On each video page, YouTube provides the code snippet necessary to embed a video on any website. You've probably also noticed such buttons for Facebook and Twitter on many web pages: each button encourages sharing, which exposes the product to more and more people.

Another type of viral loop leverages **social networks** to attract new users to a product. In this case, a user's activities are broadcast to their social connections; often more than once. If you've spent any time on Facebook, we're sure you've seen your friends liking articles on other sites, playing songs on Spotify, or pinning content on Pinterest.

You can combine these types to make viral loops work for your product. It is instructive to think about how each of these types could possibly apply.

## Viral Math

To fully appreciate the viral loop concept (and to understand whether viral marketing can work for you), you have to do a tiny bit of math. This viral math helps you quickly identify how close you are to getting traction through viral marketing, as well as which areas you need to focus on. The two key factors that drive viral growth are the viral coefficient and the viral cycle time.

### The Viral Coefficient (K)

The viral coefficient, or $K$, is number of additional users you can get for each user you bring in.

The viral coefficient formula is:

$$K = i * \text{conversion percentage}$$

where $K$ is the viral coefficient, i is the number of invites sent per user, and conversion percentage is the percentage of users who sign up after receiving an invitation. For example, if your users send out an average of 3 invites and 2 of those people usually convert to new users, your viral coefficient would be:

$$K = 3 * (2/3) = 2$$

If you were add 100 new users in a week, you could expect them to send out 300 more invites to your site and 200 more users to sign on with you as a result. That's viral growth!

Any viral coefficient above 1 will result exponential growth, meaning that each new user brings in more than one additional user, creating true exponential growth. **Any viral coefficient over 0.5 helps your efforts to grow considerably.**

There are two variables that impact your viral coefficient. The first is the number of invites (i) that each user sends out. If you can increase the average number of invites that each user sends out, say from 1 invite per user to 2, you will double your viral coefficient. To push this number up as high as you can, consider including features that encourage sharing such as posting to social networks.

The second variable is the conversion percentage. If your product is being shared but not generating new users, you won't go viral. As with invites, if you double your conversion percentage (by doing things like testing different signup flows), you double your viral coefficient. The best signup flows reduce friction by making things simpler, such as cutting out pages or sign up fields. For example, the conversion steps for a standard web application often involve clicking on a link and filling out a form to create an account. In that case, you could break the conversion percentage into two percentages.

$$K = i * \text{conversion percentage} = i * \text{click-through percentage} * \text{signup percentage}$$

When you break out conversion percentage in this way, you can determine the weakest part of your equation and focus on it. Your click-through percentage may be great, but your signup percentage may be sub-par. This makes it clear what to focus on – the area where you can make the biggest positive impact.

**Viral Cycle Time**
Viral cycle time is a measure of how long it takes a user to go through your viral loop. For example, if it takes an average of 3 days for invites to convert into users, your viral cycle time is 3 days.

Two viral loops with the same viral coefficient but different viral cycle times will end up with dramatically different outcomes: the shorter this time, the better. Viral cycle time explains the explosive growth of a company like YouTube, whose cycle times can occur in a matter of minutes – someone sees a video, clicks on it to go to the site, then copies the link and send it to friends.

**Shortening your viral cycle time drastically increases the rate at which you go viral, and is one of the first things you should focus on improving if using this channel.** To shorten it, create urgency or incentivize users to move through your viral loops. Additionally, make every step in your funnel *as simple as possible* to increase the number of users that complete it. That's why YouTube provides embed codes for each video: to make it simple for any user to add videos to their site or blog.

## Viral Strategy

To pursue this traction channel effectively, **you need to measure your viral coefficient and viral cycle time from the start**. Consider those measurements your baseline. Then, you need to get your viral coefficient up and viral cycle time down to levels that yield enough new users to produce steady growth for your business.

We suggest running as many A/B tests as you can. Best practice suggests focusing for weeks at a time on one major area (say your signup conversion rate), trying everything you can think of to improve that metric, and then moving onto another metric that needs improvement as you run out of ideas. Andrew notes that this process can take time:

*"Even expert teams will take 1–2 engineers working 2–3 months, minimum, to implement and optimize a new viral channel to the point where it's growing quickly without any ad spend. Once it gets going though, it becomes easier to incrementally improve and grow the product. You need a strong strategy, and need to spend considerable time and resources to get something going.*

*As you come up with your initial strategy for viral loops, create a simple dashboard of what needs to go up to be viral. Understand how new users end up helping you acquire more new users and do a lot of A/B tests (several per week) to try and improve the metrics."*

## Goals and Compromises

It is important to articulate your company's primary goals when formulating your viral strategy. Is it to grow the total number of users? Grow revenue? Profits?

If your goal is to grow your user count as quickly as possible, trimming down the signup process seems like a no-brainer as it will increase your conversion. However, if you want to grow paying customers for a B2B product, it may make sense to require credit card information when they sign up. Although this will increase the number of potential users who leave during the registration process, it may result in a higher percentage of registered customers who are likely to pay after their trial expiration – just be sure to test this!

## Loop Design

Once you have determined your goals and calculated baseline numbers, you will want to map out every aspect of your viral loop. How many steps are in the loop? What are all the ways people can enter into the loop (landing pages, ads, invites)?

Draw a map of the entire process and try cutting out unnecessary steps (extra sign up pages, unnecessary forms or fields to fill out, etc.) and increase areas or mechanisms where users can send out invitations. Doing so will improve your viral equation by increasing your invites sent and your conversion percentage.

We interviewed Ashish Kundra, founder of Indian dating network myZamana, about the effectiveness of sharing mechanisms. He said that there are numerous viral mechanics you can build into your product, but to be really successful users need to like and repeatedly use the product.

To drive usage, myZamana sends targeted emails to users based on actions they take on the site. As people use the site, their actions generate invitations to other users (e.g. "Mark liked you!"). The more people use the product, the more notifications are sent out.

## Viral Tactics

### Distribution Mechanisms

The most common viral distribution mechanisms are email and social media platforms. However, new mechanisms are constantly opening up in the form of new consumer applications. You should be looking out for (and experimenting with) such new mechanisms if you're focused on viral as one of your primary traction channels.

Experimenting with newer sites like Instagram, Snapchat and Pinterest for distribution could be very effective right now. As we said in the introduction, marketing techniques are constantly becoming more saturated. When looking at a medium to use for your viral campaign, Andrew gave pointers on how to choose a viral distribution platform:

*"The ideal thing is to pick something that's not too old (email address books/invites) and not too new as to require too much integration, but rather, in the middle."*Andrew uses the following framework to structure his thoughts about the viral strategies a startup should apply:

*"How do you give users value, and how are they communicating or sharing already? In an enterprise, people collaborate over wikis. Buyers and sellers of collectibles transact over eBay. Understanding how people are already doing things today gives you a leg up in understanding how you might help them do that better.*

*You just want to help people do what they already want to do. After you understand how they are already sharing, collaborating or communicating, figure out how your product can make that better.*

*And then work out the flow of how a new user can spread your product to another set of new users, who then continue propagating it. Then optimize."*

### Effective Invitations

A non-user's first exposure to a product often occurs when a current user sends an invitation. The non-user will then have to decide what to do with the invitation or whether it's worth her time to even open it. Your goal in designing these invitations is to get potential users to engage with the invite and follow the link (or take the next step) that the invitation contains.

Invitations that work best are short and succinct. Sign up for the most viral services you can think of and you'll see what we mean. Additionally, personal hooks really help. As an example, here is an invitation email Quora (a popular question and answer site) has used.

C1. Accepts Invite                    From Quora.com

From: Quora <noreply@quora.com>
Subject: **Stephan Orme shared a question from Quora with you**
Date: February 17, 2011 9:39:09 AM PST
To: t

Stephan Orme sent you a message from Quora.com:

Stephan Orme said:

I want to share the following question with you: "What are some great examples of virality design patterns?"

To see this question, visit:
http://qr.ae/wnkE

Thanks,
The Quora Team

To disable all email from Quora, visit the following link:
http://www.quora.com/l/7RhiUInR

Good subject: has who from and what

Personal message

What's being shared

Link to view content, weak sell

Opt out of future messages

People are overloaded with information about services they don't use. This makes many people hesitant to sign up for a product they have not experienced themselves. However, viral growth is impossible if you have a low signup percentage because then you have no chance of a decent viral coefficient.

For this reason, some startups like Quora allow people to use portions of their product without signing up. This allows potential users to test-drive the product without making any sort of commitment. However, this is again something you need to test for your product.

**Effective Conversion Pages**
Conversion pages work best when they use the same messaging as the invitations that preceded them. For example, if in the invitation you say so-and-so referred you to this product, you can put the exact same message on the conversion page. It really helps in both cases (invitations and conversions) to think about the psychology of the new user. You will want to run tests to help you find out *why* people are deciding to use your product. **Understanding exactly why people are clicking on your links and signing up (e.g. curiosity, obligation, etc.) will help you think of better ways to improve your viral loop.** Surveys, sites like usertesting.com and asking users directly are great ways to uncover this psychology.

**Things to Test**
Here are some of the more common items to test and optimize:

- Button vs. text links

- Location of your call to actions

- Size, color, and contrast of your action buttons

- Page speed

- Adding images

- Headlines

- Site copy

- Testimonials

- Signs of social proof (such as pictures of happy users, case studies, press mentions, and statistics about product usage)

- Number of form fields

- Allowing users to test the product before signing up

- Ease of signup (Facebook Connect, Twitter login, etc.)

- Length of the signup process (the shorter you can make the process, the higher your conversion percentage will be)

First focus on changes that, if they worked, would result in a 5–10x improvement in a key metric. This could be something like an entirely new email auto-responder sequence, a new website design, or a new onboarding flow. Once you've made big changes, then optimize.

**Almost no optimization is too small to test**: even changing one word in a headline can have a significant impact. Because viral growth compounds, a 1% improvement can make a big difference over the long-term.

### Viral Pockets
With all viral (or near-viral) growth, there will be subgroups of users growing far more rapidly than your total userbase. We call these subgroups viral pockets. Figure out if you have viral pockets by calculating your viral coefficient on distinct subsets of your users, such as those from a particular country, age group, or other trait.

For example, you may be taking off in Indonesia while not doing as well in Australia. Once you find a viral pocket, you may want to cater to this group by optimizing text in their native language or some other way that will improve their experience.

**Seeding**

Since most viral loops are not self-sustaining, you need a constant stream of new users entering your viral loop. This process is called seeding. When seeding new users for your viral loop, you're looking for people in your target audience who have not been exposed to your product. SEO and online ads (covered in later chapters) are good, inexpensive candidates for seeding.

## Viral Mistakes

Because of the potential to acquire free customers, many startups try to go viral. Andrew mentioned he sees companies making the same mistakes:

- *"Products that aren't inherently viral trying to add a bunch of viral features*

- *Bad products that aren't adding value trying to go viral*

- *Not doing enough A/B tests to really find improvements (assume 1–3 out of every 10 will yield positive results)*

- *Not understanding how users are currently communicating/ sharing, and bolting on "best practice" strategies (Just add Facebook "like" buttons!)*

- *Not getting coaching/guidance from people who've already done it*

- *Thinking about virality as a tactic rather than a deep part of a product strategy"*

As he told us, the best way to figure out the right kind of loop to build is simple: copy those who have done it before.

*"The easiest way, for a beginner – copy someone else's viral loop until yours starts to work in a similar way. Copying someone else's loop down*

*to the detail is important, including text copy, etc. These are the things that drive performance.*

*Make it something that the user wants to do, because it creates value from them. Skype with no contacts is useless – so by helping people import their address books and invite people, you're doing them a service."*

Even if you cannot truly go viral, you can still use this channel to spur rapid growth by compounding your efforts on other traction channels. If you are getting a steady stream of new users through other channels, build a viral loop to bring in more and more users to compound such growth.

## Takeaways

- There are several types of viral loops including word of mouth, inherent, collaborative, communicative, incentives, embedded and social. Startups can combine and change types over time, but generally these loops need to be built into the product to work successfully.

- The viral coefficient is the number of additional users you can get for each user you bring in. Your viral coefficient is calculated by multiplying the number of invites sent per user by the average conversion percentage of those invites.

- A viral coefficient over 1 indicates true exponential growth. You should shoot for a viral coefficient over 0.5, which will yield strong growth effects.

- Viral cycle time is a measure of the time it takes a user to go through your viral loop. You should shorten this time so that more users will complete your viral loop faster, resulting in faster growth.

- Successful viral strategy involves constant testing, measurement, and trying new things. It is a numbers and creativity game. No test is too small, as small changes can have big effects over time.

- Viral loops that work well often have simple components.

See our viral marketing resources and discuss this traction channel with us and other startup founders on our forum:

http://tbook.us/viral

# CHAPTER 7

# Public Relations (PR)

Public relations (PR) traditionally refers to a company's public messaging of all kinds. In this chapter we focus on getting coverage from traditional media like news outlets, newspapers and magazines. Unconventional PR (like stunts and contests), content marketing, and targeting blogs are all related to PR (and can be magnified via this channel), but are covered individually in other chapters.

Starting out, an article in TechCrunch or a feature in *The Huffington Post* can boost your stature in the eyes of potential users, investors, or partners. These mentions lead to larger features in news outlets like *The Washington Post* or *The New York Times,* which can move the needle for you in a matter of days.

## How Media Works

Startup founders are often unsure about how to get press. The first step is to understand how Internet-driven media works. Ryan Holiday, former director of marketing at American Apparel and bestselling author of *Trust Me, I'm Lying,* gave us a quick introduction (emphasis added):

*"The news has fundamentally changed. Think of The New York Times. When they decide to publish an article about you, **they are doing you a huge favor**. After all, there are so many other people they could write about.*

*There are a finite number of spots in the paper. Blogs are different, as they can publish an **infinite** number of articles and every article they publish* *is a chance for more traffic (which means more money in their pockets). In other words, when Business Insider writes about you, **you are doing them the favor.***"

Most sites make their money from advertisements, so they want to drive as many page views as possible. If you have a fascinating story with broad appeal, media outlets now *want* to hear from you because you will drive visits and *make them more money*. This is why sites like *The Huffington Post* now churn out hundreds of articles a day: it drives page views, which allows them to charge more to advertisers.

There has also been a shift in how the top media outlets operate (CNN, *The New York Times*, the *Today Show*, etc.). These organizations now scour smaller outlets for captivating stories they can present to a wider audience. As Ryan says:

*"It's better to start smaller when targeting big media outlets. For them, the direct approach is rarely the best approach. Instead, you approach obliquely. So, you find the blogs that TechCrunch reads and gets stories ideas from. Chances are it will be easier to get that blog's attention. You pitch there, which leads* The New York Times *to email you or do a story about you based on the information [they've seen] on the news radar."*

This means you no longer have to pitch CNN directly if you want to get on TV. Instead, you can pitch smaller sites (ones that are easier to get coverage from) whose content is often picked up by larger media outlets. If you tell your story right, you can create buzz around your company and capture the attention of larger sources. Next thing you know, you can put "As seen on CNN" on your website.

In other words, stories and other content now filter *up* the media chain, rather than down. Ryan again:

*"Blogs have an enormous influence over other blogs, making it possible to turn a post on a site with only a little traffic into posts on much bigger sites, if the latter happens to read the former. Blogs compete to get stories first, newspapers compete to 'confirm' it, and then pundits compete for*

*airtime to opine on it. The smaller sites legitimize the newsworthiness of the story for the sites with bigger audiences."*

Tech startups frequently get exposure this way. Sites like TechCrunch and Lifehacker often pick up stories from smaller forums like Hacker News and reddit. In turn, *The New York Times* often picks up content from TechCrunch and wraps it into a larger narrative they're telling.

The DonorsChoose.org story is an example of the modern-day media chain in action. DonorsChoose is a site allows teachers to raise money for classroom projects (e.g. to buy a digital microscope for a science class). After September 11, many teachers in New York City were using the site to raise money for projects related to 9/11. The site received coverage in several local outlets about this effort, and soon got the attention of *Newsweek*.

The *Newsweek* story about teachers using the DonorsChoose platform to fund their projects received some attention, but nothing major. Then Oprah happened.

One of Oprah's people saw the article on Newsweek and decided to name DonorsChoose as one of Oprah's favorite things for 2010. This national attention from Oprah led to sponsorship from the Gates Foundation and a major uptick in donations.

## How to Pitch for PR

Though media outlets are increasingly on the lookout for good stories, there are still challenges to getting exposure. Tens of thousands of companies are clamoring for media coverage. Jason Kincaid, a former reporter at TechCrunch, told us that he got pitched over 50 times each day.

What gets a reporter's attention? Milestones: raising money, launching a new product, breaking a usage barrier, a PR stunt, big partnership or a special industry report. Each of these events is interesting and noteworthy enough to potentially generate some coverage.

Jason advises bundling smaller announcements together into one big announcement whenever possible. Breaking a useage barrier is great. Releasing a new version is noteworthy. But releasing a new version *and* breaking a usage barrier in the process is even more compelling.

## Pitch Templates

Below is an email pitch Jason Baptiste sent to TechCrunch just before launching PadPressed, his startup that helps blogs look better on iPads. It's a solid example of a good pitch – short, to the point, contains clear contact information, and links to a product demo. He even mentions he's happy to do a product giveaway, which makes this pitch even more attractive.

**Subject:** Exclusive for TC: Launching PadPressed – make any blog feel like a native iPad app

*Hey Mike,*

*Launching PadPressed tomorrow at noon EST and TC gets free reign on an exclusive before then. PadPressed makes any blog look and behave like a native iPad app. We're talking accelerometer aware column resizing, swipe to advance articles, touch navigation, home screen icon support, and more. We've built some pretty cool tech to make this happen smoothly, and it works with your existing layout (iPad layout only activated when the blog is accessed from an iPad). Okay, I'll shut up now and you can check out the demo links/feature pages below, which are much more interesting than my pitch.*

*PS – Would also be happy to do giveaways to TC readers. Thanks again and feel free to reach out if you have any more questions (Skype, phone, etc. listed below).*

**Video Demo:** *http://vimeo.com/13487300*
**Live demo site** *(if you're on an iPad): jasonlbaptiste.com*
**Feature overviews:** *http://padpressed.com/features*

*My contact info:* *j@jasonlbaptiste.com , Phone: 772.801.1058, Twitter:* *@jasonlbaptiste, Skype: jasonlbaptiste*

 *–jlb*

*772.801.1058*

Every pitch can be further improved, and Jason Kincaid had some suggestions to make this pitch even better. He said the email comes across as a "wall of text," something busy reporters who receive hundreds of emails get tired of seeing. He also mentioned that the timing of the launch is unclear. **Be succinct and clear.**

When pitching to any media outlet, it's your job to create an angle that makes your story compelling. If you can craft a narrative (e.g. how we just doubled our userbase through x, y, and z) and present it well, you greatly increase your chances of getting a story.

A good angle makes people react emotionally. If it's not interesting enough to elicit an emotion, you don't have a story worth pitching. Furthermore, your story should provoke a feeling in readers that makes them want to share it with others. As Ryan said, "satisfaction is a non-viral emotion" – you want readers to *do* something after reading your piece, not just feel satisfied.

For example, Ryan worked with a client who wrote a book about how Wall Street operates. The book contained technical details about high-frequency stock trading and its impact on the economy. However, when they pitched the story, they focused on the book's implication that the stock market is essentially rigged.

This pitch resulted in much more press than a book about the stock market typically would receive. Rather than leaving it up to reporters to figure out how to position the story, they now had a story "handle" they could grab when writing about the book. This handle created a strong reaction after readers learned that the stock market is essentially a fixed game, which drove conversation around the book.

Once you pick an angle that works, Ryan offered this template email he's used to pitch reporters successfully:

**Subject:** Quick question

*Hey [name],*

*I wanted to shoot you a note because I loved your post on [similar topic that did a lot of traffic]. I was going to give the following to our publicist, but I thought I would go to you with the exclusive because I read and really enjoy your stuff. My [company built a userbase of 25,000 paying customers in two months without advertising / book blows the lid of an enormous XYZ scandal]. And I did it completely off the radar. This means you would be the first to have it. I can write up any details you'd need to make it great. Do you think this might be a good fit?*

*If so, should I draft something around [their average] words and send it to you, or do you prefer a different process? If not, I totally understand, and thanks for reading this much.*

*All the best,*

*[Your Name]*

## PR Tactics

After coverage in small blogs, you're in a good position to start pitching larger and more influential media. **Follow influencers in your industry and reach out to the blogs they often link to.** Those blogs are likely the starting points for much of the news that filters up to the larger outlets.

Have a goal in mind when you choose where to focus your pitching efforts. If you want funding, or if your target users are the startup/tech crowd, TechCrunch and re/code are good places to go. If you are trying to get users outside of the tech world, pitch the blogs and news outlets your users frequent.

## Starting Out

As we discussed earlier, the best way to get PR is to start small. A good first step is using a service like Help A Reporter Out (HARO), where reporters request sources for articles they are working on. While you won't be the centerpiece of the article, assisting a reporter this way will get you a mention in the piece and help establish your credibility. Plus, you can put the logo of another publication on your site or deck.

Another starting point is to offer reporters commentary on stories related to your industry. One of your (many) jobs as a startup founder is to stay on top of market trends. If you have a good feel for the pulse of your market, you can follow-up with insights on specific stories and let them know that you are available as an industry source.

You can also use Twitter to reach reporters online. Almost all reporters have Twitter accounts and you'd be surprised at how few followers many of them have. This limited audience can work to your advantage: you have a better chance of standing out when you contact them. Staying in contact with them over Twitter then gives you a leg up when you eventually reach out to them with your more formal pitch. This is exactly how DuckDuckGo was recognized as one of Time Magazine's top 50 sites in 2011: Gabe interacted with the reporter on Twitter and was then included in the feature piece (see the resources for the full story).

## Amplifying

Once you have a solid story, you want to draw as much attention to it as you can. Here are a few ways to do it:

- Submit a small story to community sites (like Digg, reddit, Hacker News, etc.) with larger audiences.

- Share it on social networks to drive awareness, which you can further amplify with social ads (see chapter 10).

- Email it to influencers in your industry for comment. Some of them will share it with their audience.

- Ping blogs in your space and show that you have a story that's getting some buzz. These writers may then want to jump in themselves to cover you.

Once your story has been established as a popular news item, drag it out as long as you can. Email blogs that covered the story (as well as ones that didn't) and offer an interview that adds to the original story. "How We Did This" follow-up interviews are popular.

**Fundraising**
In addition to driving traffic, PR can have a substantial impact on your fundraising efforts. Ryan Holiday talked about this in our interview:

*"PR has a huge impact on early stage startups... Funding is obviously very important. But, funding is essentially gambling. You're saying 'I think this unproven person deserves two million dollars of my money to build a business that may or may not succeed, and if it does succeed we need to find a buyer who will pay even more to take it off our hands'. There are so many things that can go wrong.*

*When people gamble, but they don't tell themselves they're gambling (as investors do), they need information to justify their decisions, and they need social proof and examples and evidence that they're doing the right thing. They already know if they want to invest in you or not, and they're looking for confirmation that they made the right call. Press is one of the single most effective things for pushing people over the edge and confirming they did the right thing."*

Jason Kincaid also talked about the role of press as a form of social proof in our interview:

*"The reason why you tend to see a lot more coverage focused on funded companies isn't so much that reporters care about whether you're funded. It's that it's easier to pick out the companies that are interesting to write about."*

**PR Firms**

As your startup grows you may choose to hire a PR firm or consultant to help you with this traction channel. This is especially true if you chose to focus on PR as your traction channel.

A good PR firm can help you:

- Figure out the best messaging and positioning to the press.

- Unify your messaging to the press.

- Do a lot of the legwork in setting up press engagements (especially bigger media tours and events).

- Break into outlets that are traditionally harder to break into like broadcast TV and radio, where relationships with reporters and producers are harder to form.

However, before making the choice to focus on PR, exercise caution; many of the (print) reporters we talked to said they ignore almost all pitches from PR firms but do listen to most founders. They're also expensive: if you're just testing this channel you can often do it faster and cheaper yourself.

## Conclusion

Getting media attention is a lot like launching a product in general: it's your job to craft an amazing story and make sure that people pay attention. In the best scenario, PR can vault you from being unheard of to a market leader essentially overnight.

## Takeaways

- Press stories often "filter up," meaning major news outlets are often looking to major blogs for story ideas, which are in turn are looking at smaller blogs and forums. That means if you can target the right smaller sites and generate buzz on them, you can increase your chances of getting picked up by bigger publications.

- Figure out the specific reporters covering your startup's market and focus on building real relationships with them (e.g. read what they write, comment, offer them industry expertise, follow them on Twitter, etc.).

- Reach out to reporters only when you have newsworthy milestones to share, and package those milestones in a compelling emotional story. When you do make a pitch, keep it short and sweet!

See our public relations resources and discuss this traction channel with us and other startup founders on our forum:

http://tbook.us/pr

# CHAPTER 8

# Unconventional PR

Do you remember Richard Branson wearing a space suit to announce the launch of Virgin Galactic? How about the Old Spice man filming YouTube videos for people who tweeted at him? Or the car service Uber delivering cupcakes and kittens to employees who wanted a break from work? PR stunts like these are not only amusing, but also a proven way to generate press coverage and buzz.

Unconventional PR doesn't suffer from the crowding that other more popular traction channels face. Nearly every company attempts traditional PR, but few focus on stunts and other systematic ways to get buzz. We talked with David Hauser, founder of Grasshopper.com and Chargify.com, to hear how he systemized this traction channel, why he hired two full-time employees to focus on it, and the impact it has had on growth.

## Two Types of Unconventional PR

There are two different types of Unconventional PR. You're probably familiar with the first type: the **publicity stunt**.

A publicity stunt is anything that is engineered to get media coverage. Richard Branson made his press conferences as outlandish as possible (dressing like a woman, driving a tank through the streets) to get the media talking about whatever Virgin was launching. By creating a spectacle around every one of his product launches, Richard Branson turns uninteresting product launches into national headlines.

The second type of Unconventional PR is **customer appreciation:** small, scalable actions (like sending cookies or hand-written notes to customers) that increase goodwill and word of mouth.

Small gestures like these turn your customers into evangelists, which leads to an increase in organic growth. And they add to your unique image and story, both key elements in building a strong brand.

## Publicity Stunts

When done right, **publicity stunts can propel a startup from ano-nymity to national recognition in an instant.** For example, let's look at the story of Half.com.

For their launch, the team at Half.com realized they needed to do something big to get on the national radar. They spent weeks thinking of ways they could get the recognition they wanted. Eventually, they came up with the idea to rename a town. And, in one of the most well-known startup PR stunts, they pulled it off. For one year, the little town of Halfway, Oregon, was known as Half.com.

Founder Josh Kopelman launched Half.com on the *Today Show* with the mayor of Halfway, Oregon. This stunt had everything tradition-al media loved in a piece. It was unique, surrounded the launch of a high-potential new startup, and told a story about how the company was creating jobs in a small town (they hired several residents).

Half.com received coverage from *The New York Times,* PBS, *The Wall Street Journal,* and hundreds of other publications as a result of this stunt. They launched in late 1999, before the days of ubiquitous email and social media. Even without these sharing tools, this campaign re-ceived more than *40 million* impressions and gave them a strong cus-tomer base right out of the gate.

WePay, a web payments startup, pulled another popular stunt at Pay-Pal's annual developer conference. Rather than marketing to PayPal's customers traditionally, they placed a 600-pound block of ice at the conference entrance.

*"PayPal freezes your accounts: Unfreeze your money"*

At the time, PayPal had been criticized for freezing some of their customers' accounts. With this little stunt, WePay shifted the conversation to focus on these frozen accounts – at PayPal's own conference!

This stunt led to thousands of signups. It also put WePay on the map as a viable alternative to PayPal when few people knew they existed.

As another example, DuckDuckGo (Gabriel's search engine) bought a billboard in Google's backyard highlighting its privacy focus. They then used the billboard to get national press stories in *USA Today*, *Wired*, and many other media outlets. The reactions from this stunt alone doubled their userbase at the time.

### Viral Videos

Blendtec is a blender manufacturer located in southern Utah. In 2007, they realized they needed to increase their brand awareness but didn't have a large marketing budget. They decided to create a series of videos called "Will It Blend?" In these videos, Blendtec's CEO stood by one of their blenders and blended items like a rake, golf balls and even an iPhone.

The videos took off shortly after posting the videos to YouTube. The iPhone video alone has received over 8 million views, and the Will It Blend? series has become one of the 100 most-viewed on YouTube. All for a company that makes blenders!

Dollar Shave Club, a subscription shaving startup, got similar attention for their launch video titled "Our Blades are F\*\*king Great." It also has millions of views on YouTube and was the main source of the 12,000+ customers they acquired within two days of launching. The video was also shared 31,000+ times on Facebook, received over 9,500 comments, 12,000+ Likes, and more than 16,000 Tweets.

The company benefitted in other ways as well. Though Dollar Shave Club has been around for just a short while, at the time of this writing in 2013 it already ranks as the third result for the Google search "shave." This ranking is largely thanks to the 1,500+ sites that linked to their video. The video led to features in *Forbes*, *The Wall Street Journal*, and *Wired*.

## Customer Appreciation

On the other end of the unconventional PR spectrum is the more sustainable, systematic form of this traction channel. Customer appreciation is a simple way of saying "be awesome to your customers."

### Gifts

We talked with Alexis Ohanian, founder of reddit and Hipmunk, about how he's made customers fall in love with his companies. Shortly after Alexis launched Hipmunk, a travel booking site, he sent out luggage tags and a handwritten note to the first several hundred people who mentioned the site on Twitter.

These tags were functional, cute, and led to many Tweets and pictures from customers excited to have a chipmunk as a travel companion.

Hipmunk also gave out other free swag (t-shirts, stickers, handwritten notes) to show their customers appreciation.

Alexis did the same thing at reddit. In their early days, he handed out free t-shirts with the reddit alien on the front. He personally emailed their users to thank them for spending time on the site and did everything he could to make early redditors feel appreciated for being part of the community.

David Hauser took a similar approach at Grasshopper.com. Over the past several years, he's sent customers Skittles, homemade cookies, Starbucks gift cards, books, and handwritten notes thanking them for their business. Doing these types of things has worked so well for Grasshopper that they have hired two full-time employees whose sole responsibility is to delight their customers.

**Contests and Giveaways**

Holding a contest is a great way to get some word of mouth without spending much money or engineering a large PR stunt. Shopify.com, a popular ecommerce platform, is famous for their annual Build A Business competition (and its six-figure prize). Last year, the contest drove 1,900 new customers and more than $3.5 million in sales on their platform.

Dropbox holds a similar contest with their annual Dropquest competition. In Dropquest, users who successfully complete an intellectually challenging online scavenger hunt are rewarded with online recognition, swag, and free Dropbox packages for life. In the first year of the competition, they had almost *half a million* people go through the quest.

Hipmunk has run similar events, like their Mother's Day Giveaway, when they asked users to tell them why they love their mothers more than Hipmunk. They received hundreds of submissions via Twitter and sent flowers and chocolates to the moms of the lucky winners.

For $500, Hipmunk generated a lot of attention, increased their follower count, and made several of their customers (and their moms) Hipmunk fans for life.

Hipmunk continues to use this channel, running a similar Father's Day promotion, flying customers home for Thanksgiving and hiring a cartoonist to draw "chipmunked" versions of customers' Facebook profile pictures.

For this last promotion, Hipmunk paid an artist to draw chipmunk-like images of their users based on their Facebook profiles and interests. They received over 500 requests in less than an hour and were covered by Mashable and several other popular blogs for this funny contest. In the end, their users received funny Facebook profile pictures and Hipmunk once again created a connection with their customers (and increased their Facebook fans by over 350%).

### Customer Support
Good customer support is so rare that, if you simply try to make your users happy, they are likely to spread the news of your great product.

Zappos is one of the best-known examples of a company that has incredible customer service. Rather than spend money on marketing, Zappos focuses on creating the best customer experience possible, especially with their support team. In fact, Zappos classifies customer service as a marketing investment and does not track metrics that could lead to poor customer service. For example, if the average time per phone call at Zappos is high, they do not view that as a negative. It might mean that their support team is taking the time necessary to do an outstanding job.

Zappos customer support personnel will help you however they can – whether that's assisting with returns, ordering a pizza, or exchanging workout clothes for a deep fat fryer (real example). With policies like free next-day shipping and free returns, this focus on customer happiness has made them famous among customers who rarely receive such treatment from large companies.

Dan Andrews, founder of TropicalMBA.com, mentioned that any interaction with customers is critically important. He values customer support because it's a repeatable interaction with your customers that allows you to make a positive impression:

*"It's the fourth dimension of branding, and it's the most important part. Traditionally, a brand might have been represented by ads on TV, billboards, or the football field. Now, this same branding happens on the web. It's not good enough to just have a cool logo or good positioning; what matters is consistently coming across to your market in a positive and authentic way."*

## Cost and Impact

Unconventional PR tactics can have incredible returns on investment. At Half.com, Josh Kopelman spent $70,000 and made two hires to generate hundreds of articles and over 40 million impressions. Dollar Shave Club acquired over 12,000 customers with a short video that cost $5,000. Hipmunk received thousands of Facebook Likes from a chipmunk-drawing contest that cost them $500. Blendtec increased their sales by over *500%* after starting the *Will It Blend?* series.

David Hauser told us exactly how valuable their various PR stunts were. In 2009, they rebranded their service as Grasshopper.com. Rather than issue a standard press release, they decided to send chocolate-covered grasshoppers to 5,000 influential people. With each package they included a link to a short video about how entrepreneurs can change the world.

After launching the campaign, they received coverage from major news outlets such as Fox News and were the subject of tweets by Guy Kawasaki and Kevin Rose, entrepreneurs with millions of combined Twitter followers. For $65,000, Grasshopper became a well-known brand among entrepreneurs (their target audience). They received major media coverage, created a YouTube video that was viewed over

200,000 times, were written up in over 150 blog posts, and increased the number of visitors coming from Twitter and Facebook by over 3,000%.

This Grasshopper 5000 campaign was not a result of random thinking or inspiration in the shower. Rather, when Grasshopper was going through a rebranding, David sat down with his team with the explicit goal of figuring out how they could get media coverage.

David knew he wanted to send something physical in the mail, as it would be far more memorable than an email. He also knew that they wanted to tie their company to the larger trend of supporting entrepreneurs. With these two parameters in mind, the team came up with the idea to send grasshoppers to people!

However, after seeing the bug-eyed, disgusting look of the grasshoppers, the team covered them in chocolate to make them less shocking (and tastier). With each package, they included a card that linked to a video they created, titled "Entrepreneurs Can Change the World."

The Grasshopper team did two interesting things here. First, they capitalized on current trends to get media coverage: social and political support for entrepreneurs has increased over the last few years. By creating a video that tied Grasshopper to entrepreneurship, they positioned themselves as a startup-friendly company that stood with entrepreneurs as they tried to change the world. When coupled with chocolate-covered Grasshoppers, this stunt led to stories from Fox, CBS, and other media outlets, hundreds of user-generated videos, and strong brand recognition.

After the success of the Grasshopper 5000 campaign, the team realized they needed to capitalize on the excitement around the Grasshopper brand. David and his team pulled off another successful stunt when they introduced the New Dork video. They saw viral videos were taking off, but noticed a lack of startup-themed videos.

With these thoughts in mind, they spoofed the Jay-Z and Alicia Keys song "Empire State of Mind" with a video called the New Dork.

This video received more than one million views and was mentioned by Ashton Kutcher, Mashable and TechCrunch. The Grasshopper team made a conscious decision to include references to popular publications like Mashable in their video. When the video came out, they sent them a quick note about where they made an appearance. This approach gave publications and individuals an incentive to show their audience how cool they were (by referencing themselves in the video) while giving Grasshopper additional exposure.

David's team at Chargify (another one of his startups) pulled off another successful stunt at SXSW in 2010. Rather than pony up the $10–15k SXSW sponsors normally have to pay, they did something completely different and had a big green bull run around the conference.

For $3,000, they hired a stuntman to dress up in a green bull's costume (Chargify's mascot) and get people pumped about Chargify.

Before this conference, Chargify was a virtual unknown. After SXSW attendees saw a green bull giving people high fives, doing backflips, driving a Corvette, and getting kicked out of the convention center, the Chargify team left the conference with hundreds of customers and a significant jump in brand awareness.

Of course, David's team has also had their share of flops. They've launched unsuccessful March Madness promotions, done failed ticket giveaways, tried to create videos of dancing grasshoppers, and many other things that just didn't pan out.

Even with the flops, this channel has been worth it. David told us that the majority of their marketing expenses are spent on the stunts and unconventional things they do to generate buzz.

He also engages in the customer happiness side of unconventional PR. For example, his companies will occasionally refer their customers to the press. When media outlets reach out to them, rather than use this as a chance to promote their own products, Grasshopper will often introduce a reporter to one of their customers.

As a small business, you can imagine the type of impact this action has on customer loyalty and word of mouth. *Nobody* expects to buy phone service from a company and have them pitch your startup to the press. That's exactly why it's so effective.

David has also made it a point to hold customer dinners any time he travels somewhere. If Chargify is going to Austin, they email some of their customers in Austin and invite them out to dinner. This has been one of the best ways to interact with their customers, understand how they can improve, and form real relationships with people who might otherwise be numbers in a customer database.

*Takeaways*

- A publicity stunt is anything that is engineered to generate a large amount of media coverage. They are often hard to do consistently well, but just one well-executed stunt can move the needle for your company.

- Publicity stunts need to be creative and extraordinary to succeed. However, some types that have been successful repeatedly are competitive stunts and viral videos.

- Customer appreciation is simply a way of saying "be awesome to your customers." Excelling in this area is a more sustainable way to do unconventional PR over the long-term.

- Common ways to do customer appreciation well are through gifts, contests, and customer support.

- Success in this channel is unpredictable. You should have a defined process for brainstorming and selecting ideas, but also understand that not every idea will work and prepare for that reality.

See our unconventional PR resources and discuss this traction channel with us and other startup founders on our forum:

http://tbook.us/upr

# CHAPTER 9

# Search Engine Marketing (SEM)

Search engine marketing (SEM) refers to placing advertisements on search engines like Google, where online marketers spend over $100 million *each day* on Google's AdWords platform. Sometimes the term may include search engine optimization (SEO), which is a channel we cover in chapter 12. In this chapter we just focus on paid search.

Paid search advertising (also known as pay-per-click, or just PPC) involves buying ads for keyword searches. For example, when someone searches for "leather shoes," a shoe company would bid to show advertisements next to or above the links that organically show up. It's called pay-per-click because the shoe company only pays when a user clicks on an ad.

SEM works well for companies looking to sell directly to their target customer. You are capturing people that are actively searching for solutions. The scale of search engines is so vast that this channel works for any product phase.

## SEM Terminology

Here is some basic PPC terminology you should understand before we dive in:

- **Click-Through Rate (CTR)** – the percentage of ad impressions that result in clicks to your site. For example, if 100 people see your ad and 3 of them click on it, you have a CTR of 3% (3/100).

- **Cost per Click (CPC)** – the amount it costs to buy a click on an advertisement. CPC is the maximum amount you're willing to pay to get a potential customer to your site.

- **Cost per Acquisition (CPA)** – CPA is a measure of how much it costs you to acquire a *customer*, not just a click.

For example, suppose you buy clicks at $1 and 10% of users that hit your site after clicking on your ad make a purchase. This puts your CPA at $10:

CPA = $1/10% = $10.

You are paying $10 to acquire each customer. The 10% in this equation is known as the *conversion percentage*, which is the rate at which people "convert" by taking the action you want (in this case making a purchase).

For paid search in particular this measure is calculated with the following formula:

CPA = CPC / conversion percentage.

## Case Study: Inflection

We interviewed Matthew Monahan, CEO and Co-founder of Inflection, a company that at their peak was spending six figures *per month* on SEM. Inflection is the company behind Archives.com, a genealogy site, which was acquired by Ancestry.com for $100 million.

Inflection's core technology is their aggregation and management of billions of public records. They originally chose to experiment with SEM because it can provide quick customer feedback and allowed the team to test different product features and messaging. As Matthew told us:

*"One of the things I want to really emphasize here is just how compelling SEM is as a way to get early customer data in a fairly controlled, predict-*

*able manner. So even if you don't expect to be profitable, you can decide to spend $5,000 (or $1,000, or $500) on an advertising campaign and get an early base of customers and users. It informs a whole bunch of things that are really important in terms of the basic [metrics]: conversion rate of your landing page, how well email captures are working ... if you're selling a product, what the average cost per customer is and what their lifetime value might be. Having those baseline metrics is critical for informing your strategy moving forward and determining what you need to work on."*

The Archives.com team used AdWords to drive traffic to landing pages *before* they made a big investment in building a product. Each landing page was written to test interest in a specific product approach.

For example, one landing page tested "get access to census data" while another tested "get access to your family genealogy." By measuring the CTR for each ad and conversions on the associated landing pages, they determined which aspects of the product were most compelling to their potential users and what those users would actually pay for. Matthew explains further:

*"We just wanted to learn as much as we could for as little cost as possible. So we would test different keyword segments, we would test different concepts. For example, one of the early concepts we were trying to test was whether people wanted to trace their genealogy to find as many of their ancestors as possible. We had to ask ourselves, 'are we trying to build a product experience where you can find hundreds and hundreds of your ancestors, or are we trying to build a product experience where you can go as far back as possible, like trace your family tree all the way back to the 1200s? Or, are people more motivated by finding out they're related to a celebrity or some historical figure, and therefore should we focus more on those family trees and those lineages?'*

*We didn't know what the answer was, so rather than invest a lot of money into engineering these different product solutions, we started by running simple ad copy tests and landing page tests. Simply testing head-*

*lines, like 'discover as many of your ancestors' or 'trace your family tree as far back as possible' or 'Find out if you're related to a celebrity,' you know the click-through rates on those are different. And when you run them across tens of thousands or hundreds of thousands of impressions, you're pretty quickly able to get statistical significance about what people want."*

Matthew's approach exemplifies the benefits of building traction and developing your product in parallel. Running these small tests enabled Inflection to make improvements to their product while simultaneously acquiring customers.

These tests also gave the team a clear idea of the type of product their customers wanted. When they finally built their product, they built something they *knew* their users would want, not something they *thought* users would want. When it came time to ramp up their marketing efforts, they knew their product was something people wanted.

As we said in the introduction, a good product development methodology like Lean will help you do some of this, but only takes you so far. From early tests, Inflection knew that people wanted different kinds of ancestry data. To learn which one would be the best to get traction with, they used SEM to measure which kinds of customers were mostly likely to pay, and the type of product messaging they responded to. Had Inflection simply done Lean, they may have chosen a direction only to back up and pivot later when real market feedback came in. Doing traction and product development in parallel got them to traction much earlier.

Such tests also give you a rough idea of how much it will cost to acquire a new customer. For example, if your product costs $10, and it costs you $40 to acquire a customer with paid search, SEM probably won't be a viable traction channel. Archives.com's PPC campaign broke even after just a few weeks, meaning their CPA was about equal to the amount of money they made from each customer.

Since they had such positive early results without even optimizing their landing pages and signup flows, the team realized that SEM would be a great channel for them. And it was – the Archives.com business was essentially built on paid search. They dedicated several employees and more than $100,000 a month to customer acquisition through this channel.

## Starting with SEM

The basic SEM process is to find high-potential keywords, group them into ad groups, and then test different ad copy and landing pages within each ad group. As data flows in, you remove under-performing ads and landing pages and make tweaks to better performing ads and landing pages to keep improving results.

Google's AdWords is the main platform for SEM because Google has the most search engine traffic. However, Microsoft Ad Center (with its ads running on Yahoo!, Bing and DuckDuckGo) is also growing. We will focus on Google's platform here, but the same concepts apply across all SEM platforms.

Keyword research is the first core component of a strong SEM strategy. With Google's Keyword Planner, you can discover the top keywords your target customers use to find products like yours. When you enter a term in this tool, it tells you how often your keyword (and similar terms) are searched. Other tools like KeywordSpy, SEMrush, and SpyFu are valuable for discovering keywords your competition uses to attract customers.

You can further refine this keyword list by adding more qualifying terms to the end of each base term, creating what are known as "long-tail keywords." For example, if you wanted to reach people searching for "census data," you could make that a more targeted search term by adding "1990" to form "1990 census data" or even more long-tail like "1990 Philadelphia census data." Long-tail keywords are less competitive and have lower search volumes, which make them ideal for testing on smaller groups of customers.

Keep in mind that SEM is more expensive for more competitive keywords. As such, you will want to limit yourself to keywords with profitable conversion rates. For example, Matthew's team at Archives.com started with roughly 100,000 keywords. As they refined their SEM campaigns, they cut out many unprofitable terms and ran optimized, profitable campaigns with the 50,000 or so keywords that actually converted well.

After you have keywords you want to target, it's time to run experiments on the AdWords platform. You should not expect your campaigns to be profitable right away. However, if you can run a campaign that breaks even after a short period of time (as Inflection did after a few weeks), then SEM could be an excellent channel to focus on.

## Running a Campaign

A campaign is a collection of ads designed to achieve one high-level goal, like selling shoes. You first create different ad groups. For example, if you're an ecommerce store, you might create an ad group for each product type (e.g. sneakers, loafers, etc.). You then select keywords you want your ad groups to appear for (e.g. "Nike sneakers" for sneakers).

After you've determined the ad groups and keywords you are targeting, create your first ad. When you write an ad, the title should be catchy, memorable, and relevant to the keywords you've paired with it. You will also want to include the keyword at least once in the body of your ad. Finally, you will want to conclude with a prominent call to action (e.g. Check out discounted Nike Sneakers!).

Once you set up your ads, you should use the Google Analytics URL Builder tool to create unique URLs (web addresses) that point to your landing pages. **These URLs will enable you to track which ads are converting, not just the ones that are receiving the most clicks.**

Matthew told us that **someone just starting out in this channel should begin testing just four ads.** Four ads will give you a good baseline for the performance of SEM as a whole, while still allowing you to test different messaging, demographics, and landing pages.

If a test is promising, you will keep trying to optimize your campaign to make it become profitable. Building a scalable SEM campaign can take a long time because there are so many variables to test – keywords, ad copy, demographic targeting, landing pages, CPC, and more. However, this complexity can actually work to your advantage. As you test and optimize every element of your SEM strategy, you may find opportunities for huge gains. As Matthew told us:

*"I think it's a huge competitive advantage because, even though it can feel like tinkering or incrementalism at the time, what you're really talking about is a major business improvement. Let's say keywords cost 15 cents, and you're running a website and for every click you're able to generate 13 cents. Well if you scale that, that's a losing business. If you improve ... and you get that 13 cents to 16 cents, now all of a sudden you have something that's more sustainable. And if you go from 16 to 20 cents, you're looking at 25% profit margins in terms of sales minus marketing.*

*So, a small gain, to go from 13 cents to 20 cents, is essentially a 50% gain, but it's a complete game changer in terms of your ability to advertise and your ability to scale a business. And that 50% can be achieved through optimizing all of these different levers."*

You can use tools like Optimizely or Visual Website Optimizer to run A/B tests on your landing pages. When we asked Matthew if the approach to SEM he discussed still applied to Inflection as they entered more competitive markets, he said:

*"The fundamental concepts of keyword research, market discovery, running split tests, ad tests, controlling your budget, trying to get as close to breaking even as possible, focusing on learning ... I think those things all still apply.*

*They certainly still apply to us as we build out new keyword sements. That part of the advice doesn't change, even though the dynamics are more competitive."*

## Quality Score

Each of your ads and ad groups as well as your whole AdWords account have a quality score associated with it. This score is a measure of how well customers are responding to your ads. It includes many factors including CTR and how long people stay on your site after seeing your ad.

A high quality score can get you better ad placements and better ad pricing. The quality score is Google's way of rewarding advertisers for high quality advertisements.

Click-through rate has the biggest influence on quality score by a wide margin. Because your ad's relevance to a particular keyword has the biggest impact on your CTR, you should tailor your ads to the keywords they'll appear against, either manually or dynamically (for example by using AdWords' Dynamic Keyword Insertion feature).

Several sources have mentioned that an average CTR for an AdWords campaign is around 2.0% and that Google assigns a low quality score to ads with CTRs below 1.5%. If any of your keywords are getting such low CTRs, rewrite those ads, test them on a different audience or ditch them altogether. Inflection makes it a priority to have a strong quality score, which gives them an advantage over less established companies. It also means they have more runway to optimize their ads and conversions.

## Advanced SEM

Once you have a search engine marketing campaign up and running successfully, you may want to start exploring some more advanced tools and features.

**Content Network**

When you set up a campaign, you can choose to advertise on the Google search network (traditional paid SEM), the Google content network (ads on non-Google sites), or both. For beginners and for those just testing this traction channel, the content network can be difficult to navigate. Yet once you have established profitable campaigns, you should consider expanding them to the content network, which includes millions of non-Google sites that serve Google's ads.

**Retargeting**

You should also consider luring people back to your site by retargeting through Google AdWords, or other sites like AdRoll or Perfect Audience. With retargeting, users that visit your site will see your ads elsewhere on the Internet. These ads often convert at a higher rate, as they are aimed at prospects who have already visited your site at least once.

For example, suppose you're a shoe store and a customer put some Nikes in her cart, but didn't complete the checkout process. With retargeting, you could show her an ad for that type of shoe. This personalization makes such ads particularly effective, often generating 3–10x higher CTRs.

However, be forewarned that it may feel a little creepy to certain people depending on what data you are using to retarget. People increasingly don't like ads following them around the Internet, especially those that are a reflection of activities they consider personal or private.

**Conversion Optimizer**

Another advanced tool is Google's Conversion Optimizer. It analyzes your conversion tracking data and automatically adjusts your ads to perform better. After you've been running a campaign for a while, using this tool can make your CPAs and keyword targeting better than you would be able to on your own.

If you decide to use the Conversion Optimizer, know that it can take time for Google to build a robust prediction algorithm for your campaign. Also, it cannot build a fresh campaign for you to target an entirely new group of customers. However, if you're looking to optimize a long-running campaign you've been running for a while, the Conversion Optimizer is a great way to reach your goals.

**Negative Keywords**

You can use negative keywords to prevent your ads from showing for certain keywords. You specify words that you *don't* want your ads to appear for: if you're selling eyeglasses, you want to prevent your ads from showing to people who search "wine glasses" or "drinking glasses," as those keywords will convert poorly. This technique can significantly improve your CTRs.

**Scripting**

One more advanced tactic is using programming scripts to automatically manage your ads. You might use scripts to set up new ads for certain keywords or to change existing ads. Scripts are especially helpful if you are managing a large number of ads or keywords.

If you're not yet scaling up your efforts or focusing on this traction channel, advanced tactics like these are premature. However, we suggest everyone run some SEM tests because they are straightforward, cheap to do and can give you insights into your business.

## *Takeaways*

- Click-through Rate (CTR) is the percentage of ad impressions that result in clicks to your site. Cost per Click (CPC) is the amount it costs to buy a click on an advertisement. Cost per Acquisition (CPA) is how much it costs you to acquire a customer.

- You can use search engine ads to test product positioning and messaging (even before you fully build it!).

- Do not expect your early SEM ad tests to be profitable. If you can run an ad campaign that gets close to breakeven after a few weeks, then SEM could be the traction channel to focus on.

A test ad campaign can be as little as four ads used to experiment.

- Areas you should be testing with your SEM ad campaigns include keywords, ad copy, demographic targeting, landing pages, and CPC bids. If you measure conversions effectively, you can test these variables against profitability.

- Longer keywords (known as long-tail keywords) are often less competitive because they have lower search volumes. As such, they are cheaper and so can be more profitable – you just may have to aggregate a lot of them to get the volume you need to move the needle.

- Pay close attention to your ad quality scores. High quality scores get you better placement on the page and better pricing on your ads. The biggest factor in quality scores is CTR.

See our search engine marketing resources and discuss this traction channel with us and other startup founders on our forum:

http://tbook.us/sem

# CHAPTER 10

# Social & Display Ads

The most familiar examples of non-SEM ads are the banner ads (also known as display advertising) that you see on websites all over the Internet. More recently, social ads (like those near your Facebook timeline or promoted tweets in your Twitter feed) have exploded in popularity as more people spend time on social sites.

Billion-dollar brands like Rolex, American Apparel, and other household names pay millions each year for ads that push their brand to the forefront of consumers' minds. Social and display ads are one of the larger traction channels. In total, companies spend $15 billion a year on this traction channel.

Large display advertising campaigns are often used for branding and awareness, much like offline ads. Yet display advertising can also elicit a direct response, such as signing up for an email newsletter or buying a product. On the other hand, social ads are best when approached indirectly, where you build an audience, engage with that audience over time, and eventually convert them into customers.

## *Display Advertising*

Most display advertising is run by **ad networks** that aggregate advertising inventory across thousands of sites (blogs, community sites, etc.) and sell that space to advertisers. For advertisers, they can buy ads on multiple sites through a single service. At the same time, sites can monetize their content by working with just one platform.

**Large Ad Networks**

The largest display ad networks are Google's Display Network (also known as the content network), Advertising.com (owned by AOL), TribalFusion, ValueClick, and Adblade. Each of these networks has access to sites that in aggregate receive hundreds of millions of unique monthly visitors. They have targeting capabilities that allow you to reach specific types of demographics, and offer a variety of ad formats like text, image, interactive, and video.

These networks are *enormous*. Google's display network alone has over 4 billion daily page views, 700 million monthly visitors, and reaches more than 80% of the *total* online audience. Mike Colella, founder of Adbeat, an ad intelligence company, told us that display ads allow you to reach a broader audience than SEM ads:

*"The interesting thing about display advertising is that somebody doesn't have to be directly related to whatever your product is to find out about it. For instance, if you're selling some sort of weight-loss product, you don't have to use terms in your display campaign about losing weight. You can use terms relating to nutrition or carbohydrates, because you know if someone starts to read about those things, they have an interest in maintaining or losing weight in some way."*

Advertising broadly like this increases the number of people who see your ads, and allows you to test them on specific subsets of this larger audience. This is a key point Mike touched on: you want to test your ads with different site demographics, different markets, and different product positioning.

Mike tests ads in groups of 5 and looks for places where conversions are below 10%. If that's the case, there's likely a mismatch between the ads and the sales page, so he either heavily tweaks or stops running them altogether. He also uses survey tools to ask users on his landing pages why they opted into an offer, and uses that information to further improve his landing pages.

## Niche Ad Networks

Niche ad networks focus on smaller sites that fit certain audience demographics, like dog lovers or Apple fanatics. One such network is The Deck, which targets the niche audience of Web creatives and enforces a rule of only one ad per page. As an advertiser, you know exactly the audience you're reaching.

Another network, BuySell Ads, offers advertisers a self-service platform for buying ads directly from publishers. In addition to buying and selling display advertising, BuySell Ads allows advertisers to purchase space on mobile websites, Twitter accounts, mobile apps, email newsletters, and RSS feeds. With their flexibility and low starting cost, BuySell Ads is an easy way to start testing this traction channel.

## Direct Ads

The last approach to display advertising is one of the simplest: go directly to site owners and ask to place an ad on their site for a fixed price. This works well when you want to reach the audience of a small site that isn't even running ads.

This approach only requires a few emails and a couple hundred dollars. In fact, this is the exact strategy Noah Kagan used at Mint. He approached bloggers whose readers likely would enjoy Mint and offered to pay $500 to put a banner ad on their site. It was one of the strongest traffic sources in the early days, and led to thousands of signups before and after their launch.

## Getting Started

To get started in display advertising, first understand the types of ads that work in your industry. Tools like MixRank and Adbeat show you the ads your competitors are running and where they place them. Alexa and Quantcast can help you determine who visits the sites that feature your competitors' ads. Then you can determine whether a site's audience is the right fit for you.

You can use all this information to target sites with similar demographics or even target the same sites with a better understanding of how much it costs to reach a particular audience.

## Social Ads

Think of the difference between search and social ads in terms of demand harvesting and demand generation. Consumers often see targeted search ads alongside their search results. For example, people who search for "grey Nike shoes" likely want to buy shoes *right now*. Therefore, shoe companies will pay to get their ad in front of such people. This is demand harvesting – individuals are looking for a product (demand), and companies pay to get their attention (harvesting).

Social ads, by contrast, work especially well for demand generation, i.e. generating interest from new potential customers. People who see these ads may not have any intention of purchasing now – they may not even be familiar with the company or its products. That's ok. The goal of social ads is often awareness-oriented, not conversion-oriented. A purchase takes place further down the line.

We interviewed Nikhil Sethi, CEO and co-founder of social ad platform Adaptly, to discuss how startups can take advantage of social ads to get traction. Adaptly gives companies one platform to manage and place social ads across many sites. Nikhil told us about the concept of **indirect response** (as opposed to direct response) in social advertising:

*"In the social context, what we're talking about is 'indirect response'. You're still focused on a sale, an install, a signup, or whatever, but the methodology to get there is different.*

*Instead of looking at every click and how it converts, indirect response says 'let's create an environment within the social context that's geared toward the specific product or service you're trying to offer, build affinity there, build loyalty there, and then migrate that audience toward some conversion element we want to occur at a later point in time."*

Nikhil's approach may seem counter-intuitive. Rather than focusing on selling more product directly (tracking click-through rates, conversions to buying, etc.), he believes social advertising works best when you take advantage of the unique characteristics of social media platforms to build an audience. Only after building this audience do you move them towards a conversion – whether through buying, using, or sharing your product.

Building an audience through social ads is more valuable than you might suspect. CareOne, a debt consolidation and relief company, conducted a study in 2011 comparing the customers they received from social ads against those they received from other channels. Here's what they found:

*"Social media connections filled out the consultation (lead-generation) form at a 179% higher rate than the typical customer. Sales? They were 217% more likely to make their first payment. For one particular problem area (people who partially fill out the sign-up form then quit), social media prospects went back and completed the form at a 680% higher clip than non-social media leads. They made their first payment at an astonishing 732% better rate."*

Users visit social media sites for entertainment and interaction, not to see ads. An effective social ad strategy takes advantage of these features without being intrusive or spammy. Social ads give companies the opportunity to start a conversation about their products with members their target audiences. One way startups can do this is by creating compelling content. Instead of directing users to a landing page, have your ad explain why you have developed a particular product, explain your broader mission, or have some purpose other than completing a sale. As Nikhil told us, this is where social advertising can be extremely effective:

*"If you have a piece of content that has high organic reach, when you put paid [advertising] behind that piece of content the magic happens. As more and more people see it, more and more people engage with it – because it's a better piece of content... Paid is fundamentally only as good as the content you put behind it. And content is only as good as how many people actually see it.*

*Content only goes anywhere if people care about it... With social, it's word of mouth on crack. You should only employ social advertising dollars when you've understood that a fire is starting around your message and you want to put more oil on it. Getting that spark started is based on what you're trying to say: startups do the opposite of this all the time where they waste tens of thousands of dollars trying to push a message that nobody cares about.*

*With social platforms, the burden of success is on the advertiser as opposed to the platform."*

Companies that succeed on social sites create compelling content. With one $5,000 video, Dollar Shave Club (mentioned in chapter 8) reached the same number of people as Gillette does in a year with their $60 million marketing budget. That's because their video was so engaging that viewers felt compelled to share it.

Creating engaging social experiences is another way to succeed on social sites. Warby Parker has done this well. They sells eyeglasses by mail, let you try them on, and then send them back for free. When you receive your glasses, they encourage you to post pictures of yourself to social sites for feedback from others. It is a fun, useful and engaging process.

As you can see, social advertising often goes hand-in-hand with content marketing (covered in chapter 13). If you've invested time and energy creating a great piece of content, spending a little bit of money to ensure that content gets wide distribution makes sense. At Airbrake, one of the companies Justin ran growth for, they promoted some of their best content on Twitter and Facebook. In one case, after spending just $15 on Twitter ads, they received hundreds of organic retweets, tens of Facebook likes and two submissions to reddit and Hacker News. In total, this $15 drove tens of thousands of visits to their site. Just a bit of paid promotion sparked a fire of organic engagement with the content (an interview with Stripe's CTO).

This tactic also works well with content distribution networks like Outbrain and Sharethrough. Each of these ad networks promotes your content on popular partner sites like Forbes, Thought Catalog, Vice, Gothamist and hundreds more. These **native ad platforms** make your content look like any other piece of (native) content on the target site. Since these sites have large audiences, using a native ad platform to target them can drive lots of engagement in just a short period of time.

## *Major Social Sites*

Here are some well-known social sites where you could advertise.

**LinkedIn** – LinkedIn's social network is made up of over 250 million business professionals. LinkedIn ads allow targeting by job title, company, industry and other business demographics, all factors you can't easily target elsewhere.

**Twitter** – Twitter also has roughly 250 million users. Twitter's ads come in the form of sponsored tweets that appear in users' feeds. They also have a Twitter cards ad unit that allows advertisers to capture user's emails who opt-in. Nikhil mentioned that one of the most effective approaches on Twitter is to turn on paid advertising around real-time events that your audience cares about (e.g. sportswear ads during major sporting events).

**Facebook** – Facebook has over one billion active users on their social network. From an advertising perspective, Facebook offers companies the ability to buy targeted ads based on users' interests, pages they like, or even people they're connected with. This granular targeting allows you to target very small groups of people. In fact, Gabriel (co-author) once ran a test campaign that targeted only his wife! The platform also allows you to reach a larger group of people through your fans on Facebook. As Nikhil said,

*"When you buy a Facebook ad, you're buying more than just a targeted fan; you're buying the opportunity to access that fan's social graph. With the proper incentives, fans will share and recommend your brand to their connections."*

An effective ad on Facebook may ask your users to like your ad, drive traffic to your Facebook page, create an incentivized Like page where your audience is rewarded for liking your page, or simply generate traffic for your main site.

**StumbleUpon** – With over 25 million "stumblers," StumbleUpon has a large potential userbase looking for new and engaging content. A recent case study showed that StumbleUpon was the #2 referrer of social media traffic, just behind Facebook. An interesting feature about this site is that ads don't surround the content on StumbleUpon – they *are* the content. When people hit the "Stumble" button, they will be directed to a paid piece of content that looks just like any other site on the network.

The downside to traffic from StumbleUpon is that its users are difficult to engage – most users are likely to click off your page as quickly as they came to it. This means you have to make sure to engage these users right away. Blog posts, infographics and video content can do well on the site.

**Foursquare** – With over 45 million users, Foursquare is the largest location-based social network. Foursquare ads can work well if you wish to engage a targeted, local population. Foursquare's ad platform is rapidly evolving but generally allows companies to send out ads hyper-targeted at particular locations or to people who have visited those or similar locations.

**Tumblr** – Tumblr is all about helping its 100+ million users discover high-quality content. Their new ad platform allows brands to create and promote sponsored posts, which Tumblr's many users can reblog and engage with.

**reddit** – With over two billion monthly page views and a thriving community, reddit is one of the most popular content sites in the world. reddit ads can take the form of sponsored links that hover at the top of reddit's pages or sponsored ads along the sidebar. The most successful reddit advertisements are controversial or funny. These types of ads encourage redditors (the unofficial name of reddit users) to engage with it by leaving comments and upvoting as if it were any other content on the site. You can also target "subreddits," which are smaller communities of redditors that focus on a sub-topic, like music or gaming.

**YouTube** – With more than one billion monthly unique visitors watching more than four *billion* hours of video, YouTube is by far the world's largest video site. On their platform, brands can create ads that show before a video is played (known as pre-roll), sponsor videos they want to drive views to, and create banner advertisements.

**Others** – There are plenty of other major sites you can target for social ads – BuzzFeed, Scribd, SlideShare, Pinterest, etc. Since these sites were established more recently, advertising on them presents an opportunity for substantial growth. As an example, Zynga (the social gaming company) took advantage of Facebook's early ad platform to spur their growth.

Now, it would be nearly impossible to grow the same way using Facebook ads; in any case, it would be far more expensive. If you run ads on the next Facebook, you can get a lot of traction for little cost.

## Conclusion

Although social ads and display advertising are two different beasts, they follow similar principles. Namely, you want to understand your audience, experiment with your message, and reach people in a memorable way. Social and display ads can make sense at any product phase, as they allow for very small or very large ad buys. This makes it an easy channel to test and one that can work well at scale.

## Takeaways

- Display ads are the banner ads you see across the Internet. They allow you to easily reach a very broad audience since those types of ads appear on most sites on the Internet. Ad networks are the easiest way to buy display ads.

- An underutilized strategy in display ads, especially in phase I, is to contact small sites directly and ask them to run your ads for a small fee.

- You can think of the difference between search and social ads in terms of demand harvesting and demand generation. Search engine ads harvest demand that exists now (as evidenced by search terms). Social ads help build awareness of products and create demand.

- The goal with social ads should be to build an audience, engage with that audience over time, and eventually move them to convert to customers. This indirect response strategy usually leads to more conversions than a direct response strategy that tries to get people to convert immediately.

- Creating compelling content (that people want to share) and/ or social experiences is the best way to build a presence and engage your audience on social sites.

- Study your competitors' ads to get good ideas for A/B tests to run on your ads.

See our social and display ads resources and discuss this traction channel with us and other startup founders on our forum:

http://tbook.us/social

# CHAPTER 11

# Offline Ads

There are many kinds of offline ads – TV, radio, magazines, newspapers, yellow pages, billboards, and direct mail. All of these can be utilized at almost any scale, from local campaigns to national ones. They are used by billion-dollar brands like Wal-Mart and by local teens looking for babysitting gigs. Even today, advertisers spend more on offline ads then they do on online.

Offline ads can be easy to test. For as little as $300, you can put out a radio ad in a market you're targeting and see how it performs. Billboards are the same way: you can buy space on one for a few hundred bucks a month, or rent one in a more prime location for many thousands.

We start this chapter with a few principles to guide your use of offline ads. Then, we cover specific tactics for each type of offline ad.

## *Demographics*

The demographics of each advertising medium are the most important factor to consider when making an offline ads purchase. For example, ads in the classified section of a newspaper will appeal primarily to an older crowd that still buys newspapers. Some questions you'll want answered are:

- What are the basic demographics (e.g. location, gender, race, age distribution) of the audience for this medium?

- What are the economic demographics of the audience (e.g. income, occupation breakdown, etc.)?

- How well does this advertising demographic match up with my target customer demographic?

You should be able to answer many of these questions by asking for an audience prospectus (sometimes called an ad kit) from whatever company is selling the ad inventory. As an example, for billboards you should receive information about the aggregate demographics of the area around the billboard, approximately how many people drive by it per day, and a sense of who those people are.

## Cost

In general, the cost of an offline ad depends on its reach. A billboard in Times Square goes for much more than one in the middle of Ohio because more people see it. Most offline advertisements work similarly.

To run cheap tests you look for **remnant advertising**. Remnant advertising is ad space that is currently being unused. For example, publications accept almost any price when selling empty inventory near print deadlines: after all, it is a complete loss for them if they don't sell that space.

Tim Ferriss, best-selling author of the Four Hour Body and the Four Hour Workweek, has said this on the subject:

*"If dealing with national magazines, consider using a print or 'remnant ad' buying agency such as Manhattan Media or Novus Media that specializes in negotiating discounted pricing of up to 90% off rate card. Feel free to negotiate still lower using them as a go-between."*

Buying remnant ad inventory can work across most offline mediums, not just in print. If you're not sensitive to location or timing, you can get substantial discounts by committing to buy remnant inventory. This can be a cheap and effective strategy to reach millions of people if you have a mass-market product. Think of those "We buy ugly houses" billboards or any of the repetitive billboards that you see all over the place: they are likely using this approach.

Thanks to the wide variety of offline mediums available, you can scale your ad buys according to your budget and product phase. Not sure if magazine ads will be a good channel for you? Buy a small ad in a niche publication and give it a test. Want to see if newspapers reach your audience effectively? Buy a few advertisements in a local paper.

Once you've established that offline ads are effective, you can save money by signing a longer advertising contract. With an up-front commitment, advertisers will give you a substantial discount.

## Tracking

Offline ads are much harder to track as compared to online ads that have tracking built-in. Successful offline tracking involves the use of tools like URL shorteners, unique web addresses and promotional codes to measure effectiveness. For example, we could create flyers that link to tractionbook.com/flyer. By tracking visits to that specific URL, we could approximate how many visits originated from our flyer campaign.

For direct response ads you can provide unique coupon codes. For example, if you have ads in a certain magazine, you could make the name of the magazine (e.g. "Wired") a promotional code. Alternatively, you can send them go to a unique URL (e.g. yourstartup.com/wired).

Jason Cohen, founder of code review company Smart Bear Software, was doing all kinds of offline advertising – magazines, trade shows, newspapers, and more – to sell his software. When people signed up, Jason included a section that asked new customers "How did you hear about us?" This question was designed to measure the efficacy of their online and offline campaigns.

Jason also included an offer for a free book on code review in Smart Bear ads. This book offer was another way to track the effectiveness of the ads. If an ad in *Dr. Dobb's Journal* resulted in a high number of book orders, then there was a high probability that the promotion worked.

## Print Advertising

Print advertising encompasses magazines, newspapers, the yellow pages, flyers, direct mail, and local directories. Among the different categories of offline ads, print trails only TV in terms of overall spending. Print advertising is appealing because it works with just about any budget and allows for precise audience targeting.

### Magazines

There are nearly 7,000 different magazines in the US, ranging from commercial publications with millions of subscribers to small trade publications with hundreds of readers.

There are three general magazine categories: **consumer publications** that appeal to the larger population (these are the ones you see on newsstands and in grocery stores), **trade publications** covering a particular industry or business, and **local magazines** that you'll see for free along sidewalks and near grocery stores.

You need to understand the reader demographics, circulation, and publication frequency of any magazine you're considering. To get this information, just ask the magazine for their **ad kit** (also known as a media package, media kit, or press kit). Or, use the magazine handbook produced by the Marketing Publishers Association to find magazines that appeal to your target market.

No matter how well you've targeted your audience, your magazine ad will not get a good response unless it is well designed. A compelling magazine ad will have an attention-grabbing header, an eye-catching graphic, and a tagline or description of the product's benefits.

Jason Cohen mentioned that the Smart Bear ads that performed well all had a strong call to action: in his case, the offer for that free book.

### Newspapers

Newspapers share many characteristics with magazines. They are published on both a national and local scale, their pricing is largely based on the circulation of a given paper, and they allow you to choose the type of ad you want in the paper.

They also have unique differences, one of the most important being that the newspaper demographic slants heavily towards the over-30 demographic. Many young people still buy magazines. Not many young people still buy newspapers. Thus, if you're selling a product geared towards twenty-somethings, you are throwing your money away if you advertise in a newspaper.

However, there are some ad campaigns that are uniquely suited for a newspaper setting. A few examples are time sensitive offers (like for events or sales), awareness campaigns (often as part of a larger marketing effort across multiple channels), and widely publicized announcements (like for product launches).

### Direct Mail

Direct mail entails any printed advertising message (ads, letters, catalogs, etc.) delivered to a specific group of consumers through the postal system.

It may surprise you to learn how effectively you can target customers through direct mail. You can build up a list of customers on your own or buy a list from a mailing organization. Simply do a web search for "direct mail lists" to find companies selling such information. Beware that buying lists can be perceived as spammy, and can be a complete waste of money if they are untargeted.

You can buy lists grouped by demographic, geography, or both. These lists often sell for about $100 for 1,000 consumer names, and a bit more for business names and addresses.

There are even direct mail services that will buy address lists, print your marketing materials, and assemble and mail everything for you. This makes sense if you're planning to do a high-volume mailing – otherwise, you're the one who has to do the printing, addressing, and mailing.

Here are a few good direct mail tactics to use if you are interested in pursuing direct mail:

- Provide a self-addressed envelope to increase the number of recipients that respond (if doing a postal direct-response campaign).

- Use handwritten envelopes and cards to increase the chances of someone opening and reading your mailing.

- Include an intriguing and compelling offer.

- Have a clear action you want the recipient to take (visit your website, come into your store, buy a certain product, sign up for an email list, etc.).

- Investigate bulk mail options with the postal service to get reduced pricing.

**Local Print Ads**

Local print ads include buying space in local publications (church bulletin, community newsletter, coupon booklet, etc.), flyers, directories, or calendars. These print ads are a good way to test print advertising because of their modest cost: just a few hundred dollars can expose you to thousands of people in a targeted area. Ads in the yellow pages are similarly inexpensive.

Unorthodox strategies like hanging flyers in areas where your potential customers visit can be a surprisingly effective way to get some early traction for your company. Obviously, doing something like this is not a strong phase III strategy – you don't see eBay hanging flyers at local garage sales.

But, it can be a cheap and easy way to get a few customers in a local area as you get started.

For example, InstaCab hired cyclists to bike around San Francisco and hand out business cards to people who were trying to hail taxis. These were well-targeted (it's a good bet that someone hailing a taxi would appreciate an easier way of getting around) and got the company some good buzz and customer adoption early on.

## Billboard Advertising

If you want to buy space on a billboard, you'll probably contact one of three companies: **Lamar, Clear Channel, or CBS Outdoor**. They are the power players in this $5.8 billion industry. If you want to get a sense of what is available in a given area, go to the websites of the above companies and contact a local representative. They will give you PDFs of local available billboards, showcasing their locations and audience.

We have some personal experience with billboard advertising. Gabriel strategically placed a billboard in the startup-heavy SoMa district of San Francisco to call out the differences between the privacy options with Google and DuckDuckGo, the privacy-focused search engine he founded.

A startup search engine calling out the big guy in their backyard – that is the kind of strong message that can get you some traction. In this case, DuckDuckGo didn't just capture the attention of the people who drove by the billboard. They also got press coverage from *Wired, USA Today,* Business Insider, and several other blogs and media outlets. That month, DuckDuckGo's userbase doubled!

What does all this cost? Gabriel's billboard cost $7,000 for a month. Billboards in less prominent locations can cost anywhere between $700–2,500 per month. Ads in Times Square, on the other hand, can run you $30–100K per month.

The cost of billboard space depends on the size of the ad, where it is located, the number of impressions your ad can provide and the type of billboard it is. Every billboard has an advertising score, known as a GRP score (Gross Ratings Points), based on the above factors. The number of potential impressions is based on the number of people in an area that could see the billboard: a full score means that a given billboard should reach 100% of the driving population during a month.

The major downside of billboard advertising is that it is difficult for people to take immediate action on what they see. It is dangerous for someone to visit a website, call a number, or buy a product while driving on a highway.

However, billboards are extremely effective for building awareness around events – concerts, conferences, or other activities coming to an area. In Las Vegas, for example, you'll see billboards touting acts and musicians performing in the coming weeks.

## Transit Advertising

Transit ads are placed in or on buses, taxis, benches, and bus shelters. Most ads of this kind can be effective as a direct-response tool because people in transit are a captive audience.

There are some transit ads, like those on the outsides of buses and tops of taxis that are more like billboards. Although they may not be effective as direct-response tools, they can still give you exposure and familiarize people with your brand.

If you want to get started with transit advertising, we suggest checking out a company that specializes in these ads like **Blue Line Media**. These media agencies can help you figure out where to advertise, how to create a memorable transit ad, and how to best measure and optimize such a campaign.

## Radio Advertising

Radio ads are priced on a Cost-per-point basis (CPP), where each point represents what it will cost to reach 1% of the radio station's listeners. The higher the CPP, the more it will cost you to run an ad on a station.

This cost also depends on which market you're advertising in, when your commercials run, and how many ads you've bought with that station. To give you an idea of what a radio ad costs, an ad running on a station for a week is often $500–1,500 in a local market, and up to $4,000–8,000 in a larger market like Chicago.

If scaling your radio buys, satellite radio is another place to consider. With over 50 million subscribers, SiriusXM can help you reach a lot of people with just one advertising relationship.

In addition to purchasing ad time, consider the cost of creating your ad. A simple 30-second voice spot can run you $300–500, whereas a professionally recorded ad (sound studio, special effects, etc.) can cost 3–10x as much. The best radio spots are entertaining and talk about an upcoming event or special promotion. Talk with a sales rep to be sure your ad is directly relevant to the radio station's audience.

## TV Advertising

TV advertisements are often used as branding mechanisms. Most of us remember famous Nike, Apple, or Wendy's commercials. When you consider that 90% of consumers watch TV, and the average adult watches 26 hours of TV per week, this is an offline channel that must be considered.

Quality is critical for TV ads. Production costs for actors, video equipment, editing, sound, sound effects, and shooting can run tens of thousands of dollars. In fact, some of the higher-end commercials you'll see can cost upwards of $200,000.

Fortunately, there are ways for you to reduce the costs of creating a TV ad. Using animation as opposed to live actors is a lot cheaper. If you do use live actors, you can recruit local film students to perform for you. Finally, just keeping the commercial as simple as possible will go a long way toward reducing costs (fewer shots, sets, actors, etc.).

In addition to the cost of creating an ad, there is the (national average) $350,000 for actual airtime. These costs make national TV campaigns tough to swallow for many small startups. However, over the last few years it's become possible to advertise on TV without spending so much money.

Local TV spots on one of the 1,300+ TV stations in the US can be an effective and reasonably priced way to make an impression. Prices for local commercials can range from $5–50 per 1,000 viewers for a 30-second time slot. As with so many other offline channels, you just have to contact the station to find out the number of viewers a station has and how much a TV spot costs.

Buying TV ads is a rather opaque process that involves a lot of negotiation, as there are no rate cards in the industry like those in print advertising. Thus, for larger media buys, you will likely want to hire a media buyer or agency to handle the many sellers out there and to ensure that you get a quality spot at a fair price.

## Infomercials

Infomercials are basically long-form TV advertisements. You've probably seen them, from the Snuggie to ShamWow, and all sorts of knives, vacuums, and workout products. Though the products and pitchmen in them frequently become punchlines, infomercials can work surprisingly well. For example, they were the main growth engine behind the rise of P90x and its $400 million in sales.

Traditionally, products in the following categories have used infomercials to gain serious traction:

- Workout equipment or programs

- Body care products

- Household products (kitchen, cleaning)

- Vacuum cleaners

- Health products (e.g. juicers)

- Work from home businesses

Products like these require more time to showcase what they have to offer. Consider the Snuggie. In a 15 second spot, it'd be really difficult to sell you on why the Snuggie is a great product. But through 2 minute shorts, the Snuggie was able to sell millions of units.

Infomercials can cost anywhere between $50,000–500,000 to make. They can be 2 minute infomercial shorts or the more traditional 28 minute episodes. These ads are almost always direct response: advertisers want people to see it, then visit a website or call in to take advantage of a special offer. The best infomercial marketers will often test their messaging, calls to action, and bonuses by running radio ads in advance, seeing what works well, and then incorporating those bonuses and messages into their commercial.

## Conclusion

Clearly, there are lots of ways to take advantage of offline advertising. There are also a lot of variables that can impact its performance. The branding potential, cost, impact, and flexibility of this channel make it a really strong one to consider when looking at how to get traction in later phases. The best way to approach this channel is to understand that there is no guaranteed way to predict what will work. But, if you keep at it, you may end up with an effective offline advertising strategy.

As Jason Cohen said:

*"One thing I learned at Smart Bear is that I have zero ability to predict what's going to work. There'd be a magazine where I thought 'this is just some piddly magazine, surely no one reads this,' and sure enough it was cheap (due to small circulation) and it'd do terrifically! Our ROI on some of those were incredible. And you just couldn't predict, whether on circulation size or media type, how it was going to go. And, it changed over time – an ad might be good for a quarter, or a year, and then decay slowly until it wasn't valuable anymore. It was unpredictable and decayed over time: so the only thing we were left with was trying everything and measuring what worked."*

## Takeaways

- There are many types of offline ads – including TV, infomercials, radio, magazines, newspapers, yellow pages, billboards, direct mail – and most can work in any product phase.

- Target audience demographics can vary widely per advertising medium, so search for audiences that match your target customers.

- Seek out remnant (i.e. left-over) ad inventory for the highest discounts.

- You can run cheap tests by first targeting local markets, and then scale up to regional or national if warranted.

- Use unique codes or web addresses to track the effectiveness of different offline ad campaigns.

See our offline ads resources and discuss this traction channel with us and other startup founders on our forum:

http://tbook.us/offline

# CHAPTER 12

# Search Engine Optimization (SEO)

Search engine optimization (SEO) is the process of improving your ranking in search engines in order to get more people to your site. Almost all Internet users turn to search engines for answers. As Rand Fishkin, founder of the popular SEO software company Moz, told us:

*"At its base, SEO is starting with a content strategy and finding a way to attract relevant visitors through search engines. You have to intelligently design this kind of [content] and make sure search engines can find and rank that content."*

SEO allows you to amplify all of the good things you're already doing in other traction channels (PR, non-traditional PR, content marketing) and use them to bring in more customers from search engines. Though competitive, SEO can scale well at any phase, and often at low cost.

If you're new to SEO, we recommend starting with the *Moz Beginners Guide to SEO* to learn the fundamentals (you can find a link to it in the resources). Instead of the basics, we'll be covering strategies and tactics for this traction channel.

## *Two SEO Strategies*

In SEO, there are two high-level approaches to choose from: **fat-head** and **long-tail** strategies. Both refer to different parts of the Search Demand Curve.

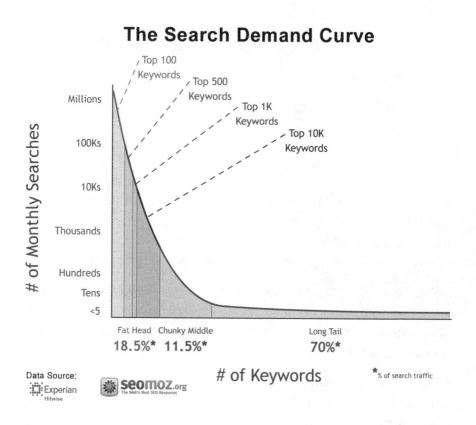

A fat-head strategy involves trying to rank for search terms that directly describe your company. For example, a toy company that specializes in wooden toys might try to rank for "wooden toys." With regards to the figure above, this strategy means working in what is labeled the "Fat Head" and the "Chunky Middle."

On the other hand, a long-tail strategy involves trying to rank for more specific terms with lower search volumes. That same toy company might try to rank for searches in the "Long Tail" like "poisonous chemicals in wooden toy blocks" or "wood puzzles for 3 year olds." Even though these searches have lower volumes, in the aggregate they account for the majority of all searches.

When determining which strategy to use, you should keep in mind that the percentage of clicks you get drops off dramatically as you rank lower on a search results page. Only about ten percent of clicks occur beyond the first ten links, so you want to be as high up on the first page as possible. In other words, **your ability to rank on the first page should be a deciding factor in deciding whether to pursue a particular SEO strategy at all.**

## Fat-head SEO Strategy

The best way to determine if a fat-head SEO strategy is worthwhile is to research what terms people use to find products in your industry, then see if the search volumes are large enough to make it a worthwhile growth opportunity.

Google currently provides a useful tool for this process called Keyword Planner (part of Google AdWords). You can type in search terms that describe your products, and then see the search volumes for these terms. You can also get keywords by looking at your competitors' websites and seeing what words they use in their homepage titles and headers.

You want to find terms that have enough volume so that it would be meaningful if you captured ten percent of the searches for that term. You don't want to spend resources ranking for a term that only gets 200 searches per month.

Optimizing your site to rank for certain key terms is great if your customers are searching for what you have to offer. If, however, your product is so new that there's no search demand for it yet, a fat-head SEO strategy will not be as effective. This is the difference between fulfilling and creating demand. Rand used Uber, the smartphone-enabled taxi service, as an example:

*"The problem with Uber is that there's not a lot of search demand for it. I mean nobody searches for 'alternatives to taxi cabs that I can hire via*

*my phone.' It's just not a thing. And this is a problem with a lot of startups that are essentially entering a niche where nothing had existed previously... There's just not search volume.*

*What works is finding the topics and the people that will be customers and building content to attract them, rather than just finding the keywords that work in Google."*

## Fat-head SEO Tactics

If you find keywords with good volume, test them by buying Google ads for your chosen keywords (see chapter 9). If these ads convert, you have an indication that SEO could be a strong growth channel for such keywords. In other words, **there is no point wasting time on terms that don't yield traction.** A common example is for ecommerce stores that rank well for terms with "free" in them – usually those visitors won't pay!

Once you've chosen some fat-head keywords with decent search volumes and that convert well, take steps to narrow your list of targeted keywords to just a few. First, go over to Google Trends to see how your keywords have been doing. Have these terms been searched more or less often in the last year? Are they being searched in the geographic areas where you're seeking customers? You can also use Google Trends to compare keywords to one another and see which have higher relative search volumes.

The next step in selecting keywords is determining the difficulty of ranking highly for them. Using tools like Open Site Explorer, determine the number of links competitors have for a given term. This will give you a rough idea of how difficult it will be to rank highly. If a competitor has thousands and thousands of links for a term you want to rank for, just realize it will likely take lots of focus on building links and optimizing for SEO to rank above them.

For example, it will be extremely difficult to rank for the term "accounting software." However, you can focus on ranking for more niche terms (e.g. "accounting software for hairdressers") by making your keywords more focused. This tactic is more in line with the long-tail strategy we'll cover shortly.

Once you've settled on a few terms that will move the needle, there are only two steps left. First, orient your site around terms you've chosen. If you are an accounting software site and "small business accounting software" is your main term, include that phrase in your page titles and main site.

Second, you want other sites to link to your site, ideally using the terms you want to rank for. The more links you can get that utilize the terms you want to rank for, the better. That is, an article may read something like "XYZ Company releases version of <u>small business accounting software</u>" (where ____ denotes the link).

## *Long-Tail SEO Strategy*

The majority of searches conducted through search engines are "long-tail" searches. Essentially, long-tail searches are sets of keywords that are highly specific – things like "owls of eastern Pennsylvania" or "private search engine." Individually, searches for these terms don't amount to much: together though, they make up 70% of all searches.

Because it is difficult to rank highly for competitive terms, a popular SEO strategy for early stage startups is to focus on the long-tail. With this approach, you bundle long-tail keywords together to reach a meaningful number of customers.

As with the fat-head SEO strategy, the Google Keyword Planner is the first way to evaluate whether a long-tail SEO strategy may be effective for you. But this time you are seeking information on more specific long-tail terms. What are search volumes for a bunch of long-tail keywords? Do people search for many variations of your keywords?

A second way to evaluate a long-tail SEO strategy is to look at the analytics software you have on your site (such as Google Analytics or Clicky). These applications will tell you some of the search terms people are using to get to your site right now.

If you do not have any content that is drawing users to your site via long-tail keywords, you have two choices. First, you could create some and see which search terms are bringing people to your site. Second, look at competitors' websites to determine if they are getting meaningful long-tail SEO traffic. Here are two signs that they are:

1. They have a lot of landing pages. You can see what types of pages they are producing by searching site:domain.com in a search engine. For example, if I wanted to see how many landing pages Moz has created targeting long-tail keywords, I could search site:moz.com and get a sense of how many landing pages they have.

2. Check out Alexa search rankings and look at the percentage of visitors your competitors are receiving from search. If you look across competitors and one site receives a lot more visitors from search than others, you can guess they have some kind of SEO strategy.

## Long-Tail SEO Tactics

Long-tail SEO boils down to producing a lot of quality content. Patrick McKenzie, founder of Bingo Card Creator and Appointment Reminder, told us how he approaches doing so:

*"You build a machine that takes money on one end and spits rankings out the other. For example, with Bingo Card Creator I pay money to a freelancer to write bingo cards with associated content about them that get slapped up on a page on the website. Because those bingo cards are*

*far too niche for any educational publisher to target, I tend to rank very well for them.*

*For 10–20 dollars per search term, you can pay someone to write an article that you won't be embarrassed to put on your website. For many SaaS [Software as a Service] startups, the lifetime value of a customer at the margin might be hundreds or thousands of dollars. So, they [articles and landing pages] don't need much traffic at all on an individual basis to aggregate into a meaningful number to the business.*

*The reason my business works is fundamentally because this SEO strategy works phenomenally well."*

In our interview, Patrick told us about his Owls of East Asia bingo cards. He uses a landing page (which we link to in the resources) that specifically discusses owls of East Asia and has a custom bingo card template just for this long-tail topic. This page has resulted in about $60 worth of business over 3 years. With a $3.50 content creation cost, it was an investment worth making. It works because few other sites on the Internet have a page specifically for people searching "owls of east Asia bingo." In Patrick's case, hundreds of these sorts of $3.50 investments for a $60–$100 return add up to big profits.

In Patrick's case, he built up a series of subpages on his site, each of which targeted a bucket of keywords he wanted to rank for. For example, there's the bingo card category for "plants and animals." This category includes pages like "dog breeds bingo," "cat breeds bingo" and (of course) "owls of East Asia bingo." For each of these subpages, he hired a freelancer to research the term and create a unique set of bingo cards and associated landing pages.

You can implement this tactic by designing a standard landing page with some basic content and a simple layout structure. Then use oDesk or Elance to find freelancers willing to churn out targeted articles for long-tail topics that your audience is interested in.

One tactic that startups have succeeded with (especially if your product involves geography in any way) is to choose several keywords and target them with geographically modified content. For example, if you want to reach individuals searching for "foreclosed homes," creating landing pages for targeting terms based on geography would work well. This means generating landing pages for searches like "recently foreclosed homes in Queens, New York City." These pages would rank more highly than a more generic landing page targeting only "recently foreclosed homes."

**Automation**

Another way to approach long-tail SEO is to use content that naturally flows from your business. To evaluate whether you could use this tactic, ask yourself: what data do we collect or generate that other people may find useful?

Large businesses have been built this way: Yelp, Trip Advisor, Wikipedia have all gained most of their traffic by producing long-tail content. This tactic was also the main channel for Gabriel's last startup, Names Database (which he sold to Classmates.com for $10 million). When people searched for old friends and classmates, they would come across the Names Database page of the individual they were searching for. These pages were automatically generated from the data that was naturally gathered by the product. After they were indexed by search engines, they sent a great deal of organic traffic from individuals doing long-tail searches for individual names.

Sometimes this data is hidden behind a login screen and all you need to do is expose it to search engines. Other times you may need to be more creative about aggregating data in a useful manner.

## Link Building

Whether you pursue a fat-head or long-tail strategy, SEO comes down to two things: content and links. The more aligned your content is with the keywords it's targeting, the better it will rank.

Similarly, the more links you can get from credible and varying sources, the better your rankings.

Getting links is often more difficult because it involves people outside of your company. Here are some ways to build links:

- PR – when you are covered by online publications, reporters will link to your website (see chapter 7).

- Product – with some products, you can produce web pages as part of your product that people naturally want to share. A great example is LinkedIn profile pages.

- Content marketing – creating strong, relevant content that people want to read, and thus share (see chapter 13).

- Widgets – giving site owners useful things to add to their sites, which also contain links back to yours.

**Link-Worthy Content**
There is a difference between creating amazing content that spreads like wildfire and hiring freelancers to write boilerplate articles for long-tail keywords. Both are valid strategies (and can work well in tandem), but there is a big difference in quality.

The point of creating amazing content in this context is to make it **remarkable enough that people actually link to it**. Rand suggests using infographics, slideshows, images and research to drive links.

Since the end goal is to get links, you'll want to target people who will link back to you. This group of people will vary depending on the product, but in general people who run blogs are big social sharers. Reporters are usually good targets as well.

Remember, this is content you *want* people to see: material that you'd be proud to email to your friends and ask them to share. Links from more reputable places like newspapers carry more weight with search engines than lesser-known sites. From an SEO standpoint, this means stronger content (that newspapers would cover) can bring you stronger links, which in turn boosts your rankings.

To sum up, **links between sites are the currency of SEO.** They are the dominant factor in a site's ranking for a given term. Open Site Explorer can tell you how many links you are getting and where they are coming from. You can also look at your competitors' link profiles to get ideas of other places to target for links.

## SEO Don'ts

In SEO, there are few big don'ts. The biggest: **don't buy links.** Buying links is against search engine guidelines and companies get heavily penalized for doing so. Similarly, trying to trick search engines in any way can lead to serious ranking penalties.

These sketchy tactics are referred to as "black-hat," as opposed to "white-hat" or "grey-hat" (on or close to the line). You want to stay squarely in the "white-hat" arena.

To be clear, black-hat tactics can work in the short-term, and therefore can seem quite attractive. However, it is hard to build a long-term sustainable business on them because at some point search engines will crack down on them and you'll lose traffic due to penalization.

## Conclusion

As Rand said in our interview:

*"I rarely see startups fail and crater because they didn't have a good idea or weren't able to execute on that idea and build a decent product. Where I see 90% of startups fail is because they can't reach their customers.*

*If marketing is the big challenge for most startups, which it is, you should prioritize content marketing to the degree to which you need to reach your market."*

This stuff works. Moz says 85% of their customers come from inbound marketing channels (search, social media, etc.) Moreover, these customers stay longer than those that come from outbound marketing channels.

Mike Volpe from Hubspot said something similar:

*"Today we have 30 people in marketing and 120 in sales all based in Cambridge, MA (no outside sales) and we attract 45–50k new leads per month, 60–80% of which are from inbound marketing (not paid). The inbound leads are 50% cheaper and close 100% more than paid leads.*

*My personal experience and industry knowledge tells me that most other SaaS [Software as a Service] companies get more like 10% of their leads from inbound marketing, and generate 2–5k leads per month in total, whereas we get 70–80% of our leads from inbound and we generate 45,000+ new leads per month."*

## Takeaways

- Two high-level strategies to approach SEO are to focus on the fat-head (short search terms) or the long-tail (longer search terms). These strategies are not mutually exclusive.

- To evaluate SEO you want to first determine if there are search terms that have enough search volume to move the needle for your company (assuming you can rank highly for such terms).

- If you identify some terms that could work, you can further qualify them by running search ads against them to test if they actually convert customers (see chapter 9).

- Your product may naturally produce good long-tail content that you can expose to search engines, or there may be an obvious way to generate long-tail landing pages by using cheap freelancers.

- Whether you pursue a head or long-tail strategy, SEO comes down to two things: content and links. Link building is often the more challenging of the two.

- One way to get quality links is to produce amazing content (see chapter 13).

- Avoid "black-hat" SEO tactics that violate search engine guidelines, especially buying links.

See our search engine optimization resources and discuss this traction channel with us and other startup founders on our forum:

http://tbook.us/seo

# Content Marketing

Think back to the last few websites you've used and take a look at their blogs. In all likelihood, they're infrequently updated, have few comments and content that isn't all that interesting.

Compare that experience to reading a well-known company blog like Moz, Unbounce or OkCupid. For each of these companies, their blog was their largest source of customer acquisition during an extended period of growth. These companies write posts that receive hundreds of comments, lead to major PR, and result in thousands of shares. Ultimately, this activity leads to new customers.

For this traction channel, we spoke with two successful entrepreneurs who have very different approaches toward content creation. Rick Perreault, founder and CEO of Unbounce, told us how Unbounce started using their blog as a marketing platform the day they started building their application. In fact, they began blogging a year before they even had a product! Unbounce's blog raised their profile in the online marketing industry and is still their main source of traction.

On the other end of the spectrum, we talked with Sam Yagan of OkCupid. The popular online dating service launched in 2004 but didn't start seriously blogging until 2009. Though they focused on other traction channels early on, OkCupid really started to take off when they focused on content marketing.

*Phase I Blogging: Unbounce*

As we discussed in chapter 4, many startups fall into the product trap – building a product before thinking about distribution. Unbounce, a company that provides simple landing page creation software, did the opposite. Rick Perreault, founder, made a full-time blogger his first hire. From day one (literally), Rick began sketching out the product features for Unbounce on the company blog.

Unbounce's target market (online marketers) are very active online. Rick therefore thought that a blog was a perfect way to attract potential customers. As he said:

*"If we had not started blogging at the beginning the way we did, Unbounce would not be here today... Our content still drives customers. Something we wrote in January 2010 still drives customers today. Whereas if I had spent money on advertising in January, that's it. That money is spent. If you invest in content, it gets picked up by Google. People find it, they share it, and it refers customers almost indefinitely.*

*By the time we launched in the summer of 2010, we were doing 20,000 unique visitors per month to the blog... It was up and running for almost a year before we launched.*

*Now, our blog is our primary source of customer acquisition. People write about Unbounce. Other people tweet about our posts... Our blog is the centerpiece of all our marketing."*

This blog-from-the-beginning approach allowed them to launch with an email list over 5,000 strong. This wasn't your typical startup product launch.

The Unbounce team relied heavily on social media to drive readers to their blog. After every post they wrote, they'd ping influencers on Twitter asking for feedback and thoughts. They also engaged with their target customers by writing useful answers on targeted forums like Quora. These efforts allowed them to build enough of an audience for their content to start spreading more organically. Though actions like this may not scale, it's OK because you're building towards a point where your content will spread on its own.

Unbounce capitalized on this early blog interest and traffic. They gave away free infographics and ebooks, like *101 Landing Page Optimization Tips*, to grow their email list. This meant that when they finally opened up their product beta, they were swamped with customers.

Getting to this point wasn't as easy as it might seem. Even with awesome bi-weekly posts about online marketing, it took six months for the Unbounce team to see results from their blog. But, once they had an audience they never looked back.

## *Phase III Blogging: OkCupid*

OkCupid is one of the most popular online dating sites in the US and was acquired by Match.com for a reported $50 million. They approached their blog differently than Unbounce, only focusing on it as a traction channel after five years of being in business.

Sam Yagan, the founder of OkCupid, mentioned that they tried several different channels before launching the blog. For example, they hired a PR firm to pitch interesting news stories based on OkCupid's data – stories such as how higher gas prices led to a lower willingness to meet potential matches or how women found Eli Manning more attractive than Tom Brady.

Using a PR firm in this manner didn't work out. However, writing these same types of stories on their own blog did. They found that presenting stories on their blog and pitching them to media afterwards was far more effective. Keeping the stories in house also allowed them to deal with controversial topics traditional PR firms were shying away from.

It wasn't until 2009 that the OkCupid team started focusing on their blog as a way to get traction. Before that they had focused on other traction channels – viral marketing and SEO – but those had stopped moving the needle.

Re-focusing on content marketing certainly paid off. Before launching the blog, growth was slow. Once they launched the blog, it increased rapidly. Take a look:

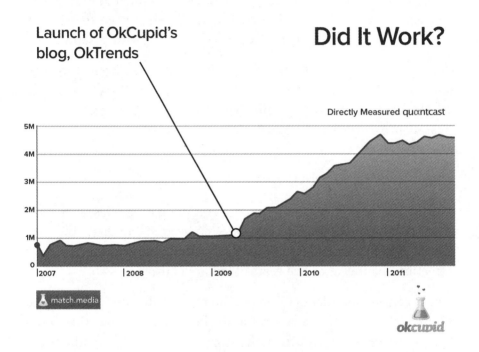

OkCupid had two goals for the blog in the early days. First, they wanted to raise their online profile. Online dating is a competitive space and in order to stand out they needed to do something unique. Second, they wanted to make it acceptable to talk about online dating. There was (and still is, to some extent) a stigma about online dating. OkCupid wanted to remove that stigma and give people a place where they felt comfortable talking about it.

Much like Unbounce, their blog was the focal point of all their marketing activities. They intentionally wrote controversial posts (e.g. How Your Race Affects the Messages You Get) to generate traffic and conversation. Each of their posts took a month to write and drew on the data they had from studying the usage patterns of their members.

Because OkCupid was a *free* online dating site, they couldn't afford to pay much to acquire users – in fact, they never did any sort of paid advertising. This meant that traction channels without per-user acquisition costs (e.g. PR, content marketing, SEO, viral marketing) needed to drive all of their growth.

Interestingly, they received much more organic PR after launching the blog than they did when working with PR firms. CNN, Rachel Ray, *The New York Times,* and many other media outlets were interested in the topics they covered.

Their blog also has major SEO benefits. When they launched it, they were nowhere near the top of search results for the term "online dating." About a year later, they were the first result for that highly competitive term.

## *Creating Strong Content*

The most common hurdle in content marketing is writers block. To overcome it, simply write about the problems facing your target customers. Presumably, you know more about the industry you're working in than your potential customers. This means that you should be able to provide insight on subjects they care about.

Every single industry has issues people struggle with. In Unbounce's case, they wrote posts about landing page optimization, PPC (pay-per-click) conversions, and so on. OkCupid's posts like "Exactly What to Say In Your First Message" addressed the concerns of online dating users in an entertaining, even controversial way.

Unbounce mixes mini-courses, ebooks, and infographics with their typical blog posts, often in exchange for a reader's email address. They've found that infographics are shared about twenty times more often than a typical blog post and have a higher likelihood of getting picked up by other online publications. For example, in 2012 Unbounce released the "Noob Guide to Online Marketing." This infographic drove tens of thousands of downloads and thousands of paying customers. One year later it was still shared on Twitter about once an hour.

Both Rick and Sam made it a point to say there's no shortcut to creating quality content. If what you're writing isn't useful to people, it doesn't matter how hard you try to spread your content on Twitter. It just won't spread.

## Growing Your Blog

In the early days, it's unlikely that your blog will see much traffic, regardless of content quality. Even Unbounce was receiving less than 800 monthly visits after six months of consistently putting out content. It took a while for them to grow to 20,000 monthly visitors.

Fortunately, there are ways to build momentum faster. Unbounce engaged in any online forum where conversations were taking place about online marketing, and did their best to contribute. They were particularly successful reaching out to influential people on Twitter. They would simply follow marketing mini-celebrities and ask them for feedback on recent posts.

One of the best methods of growing your audience is **guest posting**. This tactic is especially powerful in the early days when you essentially have no audience to work with yourself. Unbounce started doing guest posts on other popular blogs after just three months of blogging on their own.

As you move forward, monitor social mentions and use analytics to determine which types of posts are getting attention and which are not. Many bloggers are surprised at which posts do well. That is a good reason to keep a regular content schedule: it can be hard to anticipate what exactly will resonate with your audience.

## Blogs with Benefits

Quick: name three venture capitalists or ask your startup friends to do so. Many people will mention Fred Wilson, Brad Feld or Mark Suster. Why? Because they have popular blogs. They're also great venture capitalists in the same way your product has to be great to succeed. But there are plenty of other great venture capitalists that do not have similar brand recognition.

One of the best things about this traction channel is how it positions you as a leader in your space. Unbounce and OK Cupid are both great examples of how a popular blog can make a company a recognized industry leader in a highly competitive space.

Recognition as a primary voice in an industry leads to opportunities to speak at major conferences, give press quotes to journalists, and influence industry direction. It also means your content is shared many more times than it would be otherwise.

For Unbounce, some of the biggest benefits of having a strong company blog came in the form of co-marketing opportunities. When they were just starting out, they tried reaching out to popular companies to arrange partnerships (see chapter 17). These types of business development pitches were ineffective early on, but that changed after their blog started getting readership. Now, they have numerous integrations (including some major ones with companies like Salesforce), and a backlog of companies who want to work with them.

## Conclusion

Having a strong company blog can positively impact at least eight other traction channels – SEO, PR, email marketing, targeting blogs, community building, offline events, existing platforms and business development. When it works, it drives in customers like magic.

Rick put it like this:

*"[Our blog] drives search. It drives word of mouth. The blog is top of the funnel. People find the blog, and it's attached to our website. We don't market the blog, per se, but we're constantly – several times a week – releasing content that gets shared and drives people to the blog."*

## Takeaways

- A company blog can take a significant amount of time to start taking off. We think you should dedicate at least six months when focusing on this channel once you finish your small-scale tests.

- It is OK to do things that don't scale early on (e.g. reaching out to individuals to share posts) because you're building toward a point where your content will spread on its own.

- You need to create quality content to succeed in this traction channel. There is no silver bullet, but a decent approach is to write about problems your target customers have. Another approach (not mutually exclusive) is to run experiments or use data from your company to produce in-depth posts you can't find anywhere else.

- Reaching out to influential industry leaders (on Twitter, etc.), doing guest posts, writing about recent news events and creating shareable infographics are all great ways to increase the rate of growth of your audience.

- It helps to make a content calendar to make sure you're posting frequently and consistently. Keeping a running list of topic ideas can help you avoid writer's block.

See our content marketing resources and discuss this traction channel with us and other startup founders on our forum:

http://tbook.us/content

# CHAPTER 14

# Email Marketing

If you're like us, you have multiple promotions sitting in your inbox right now – coupons, referrals, sales pitches and more. This is email marketing. Many online retailers (Groupon, Fab, Jackthreads, Thrillist, Zappos) use email marketing as their primary traction channel, via sales, discounts, and newsletters.

For this channel, we interviewed Colin Nederkoorn, the founder and CEO of Customer.io, a startup that makes it easy for companies to send email based on actions your customers take (also known as transactional or lifecycle emails). In our interview, Colin shared his thoughts on how email is still the most powerful marketing channel out there:

*"If you're running a real business, [email] is still the most effective way to universally reach people who have expressed interest in your product or site. For that, it really can't be beat."*

Email marketing is a personal traction channel. Messages from your company sit next to email updates from friends and family. As such, email marketing works best when it is personalized. Email can be tailored to customer actions so that every communication is relevant to their interests.

Email can be used at all stages of the customer lifecycle: to acquire customers, build familiarity with prospects, move customers through your funnel, and retain the customers you already have. We'll go through how you can use it in each of these contexts.

## Email Marketing for Finding Customers

Before we dive in, let us give you a warning. Some companies will buy email lists and send people unsolicited email. That is the very definition of spam. Spam makes recipients angry, hurts future email deliverability efforts, and harms your company in the long run. We do not recommend it.

Luckily, there are many legitimate ways to acquire customers using email. We urge you to build an email list of prospective customers through your other marketing efforts. This is useful (whether you end up focusing on this channel or not) because a list of interested prospects is an asset you can draw on for years.

Traction channels such as SEO (see chapter 12) or content marketing (see chapter 13) can help you build your email lists. **At the bottom of your blog posts and landing pages, simply ask for an email address.** Many companies require an email address for users to access premium content, such as videos or whitepapers. In our interview with Rick Perreault of Unbounce, he stated that this tactic was the single biggest driver of their email list growth.

Another popular approach to building an email list is creating a short, free course related to your area of expertise. These mini-courses are meant to educate potential customers about your problem space and product. At the end of the course you have a call to action, which depends on your product needs. You could ask users to purchase your product, start a free trial, or share something with their friends.

If you do not want to find customers through an email list you have built yourself, consider advertising on email newsletters complementary to your product, or via other channels (SEM, social and display ads). Many email newsletters accept advertisers, and if not you can reach out directly.

## Email Marketing for Engaging Customers

Discovering customers and driving them to your site is a worthwhile goal. However, that is a just first step to building the kind of significant traction every startup is hungry for. What you really want is an email list full of *active* users.

User activation is a critical and often-overlooked component of building a successful product. The meaning of "activation" depends on the product. For Twitter, it means sending out a tweet or following five people. For Dropbox, it means successfully installing the application and uploading at least one file.

As you would expect, improving your activation rates can have a significant effect on your business. Everything gets better when your customers use and love your product. After all, if a user never gets the value of your product, how can you expect them to pay for it, or recommend it to others?

Email marketing is a great way to improve initial customer engagement. A popular approach is to create a sequence of emails that slowly exposes your new users to the key features in your product. Instead of throwing everything at them right away, you can email them five days after they've signed up and say, "Hey, did you know we have this feature?"

Use targeted emails to reach specific customers who haven't activated. These are **lifecycle emails**, where the email cycle begins when a customer signs up for your product and ends when the customer becomes active (i.e. the "lifecycle" of the customer). Colin uses lifecycle messaging to keep customers engaged in his product:

*"With lifecycle messaging, you create the ideal experience for your users when they sign up for your trial. You then create all of the paths they can go down when they fail to go through the ideal experience. And you have emails in place to catch them and help them get back on that [ideal] path."*

Let's take Dropbox as an example. If you create an account but never upload a file, you are not active. Maybe you signed up for the site but got busy and forgot about it. When this happens, Dropbox automatically emails you, reminding you to upload a file. With these targeted emails, Dropbox has increased the chance that you will return to the product and start using it.

This is what Colin meant by creating the ideal experience for your users; give them little nudges to make sure they use the product successfully. For these emails, you should determine the steps *absolutely necessary* to get value from your product. Then, create lifecycle emails to make sure users complete those steps. For those who fail to complete step one, create a message that automatically emails them when they've dropped off. Repeat this at every step where users could quit, and you will see a major uptick in the number of users finishing the activation process.

With tools like Vero and Customer.io, you can create email messages like these tailored to specific groups of users. For example, you can use these tools to send an email to users who have not activated their account within three days of signing up for a free trial. Early on, Twitter figured out that users who follow at least 5 people were far more likely to stay engaged than users who only followed 1–2 people. With this in mind, they structured their entire signup flow to get people to this activation threshold. You can also use lifecycle emails to get customer feedback. Colin sends each new Customer.io signup an automated, personal email thirty minutes after they sign up. Here's the email:

**Subject**: Help getting started?

*Hey {{ customer.first_name }},*

*I'm Colin, CEO of Customer.io. I wanted to reach out to see if you need any help getting started.*

*Cheers,*

*Colin*

He mentioned that the email receives about a 17% reply rate, which is fantastic as far as automated emails go. It opens the channel of communication between Colin and his customers. Through these replies he's learned a great deal about what wasn't working in the product, which has led to many improvements.

## Email Marketing for Retaining Customers

Lifecycle messaging is often used for customer retention as well. For many businesses, email marketing is the most effective channel to bring users back to their site.

Again, take Twitter as an example. If you're an active Twitter user, think of every email you've ever gotten from them about someone mentioning you in a tweet, a friend of yours who just signed up, or their weekly digest of popular tweets you may have missed. Each one of those emails is meant to keep you active on Twitter.

Your retention emails will depend on the type of product you have. For example, if you have a social networking product, you could send a simple email to users who haven't signed in for two weeks. Dating services often showcase profiles or mention unread messages. More business-oriented products usually focus on reminders, reports, and information about how you've been using (and getting value) from the product.

For infrequently used products, email marketing can be the primary form of customer engagement. Mint sends you a weekly financial summary that shows your expenses and income over the previous week. This keeps their product at the forefront of their users' minds and allows them to provide value even if their users aren't always signed in. BillGuard, a service that monitors your credit cards for suspicious transactions, sends you a similar report every month.

Email marketing is one of the best channels to surprise and delight your customers. Brennan Dunn of Planscope (a project planning tool for freelancers) sends a weekly email to his customers telling them how much they made that week. Who wouldn't want to get an email like that? Any sort of communication telling your customers how well they're doing is likely to go over well. Patrick McKenzie calls this the "you are so awesome" email.

Some companies send emails that show previous engagement with the product. For example, photo sites will send you pictures you took a year ago. These emails achieve both goals: they often make you feel good on an emotional level, and also invite you to come back and upload more pictures.

## Email Marketing for Revenue

The ultimate goal of any traction channel is to add customers and generate revenue. With email, there are many ways to turn your emails into money in the bank. As with any channel, coming up with the right offers, targeting and timing requires experimentation.

As we mentioned earlier, Groupon and many other companies use email to generate hundreds of millions of dollars in revenue. Patrick McKenzie, who we interviewed for SEO (see chapter 12), said his email subscribers were 70x more likely to buy one of his courses than those from other traction channels (targeting blogs, SEO, and content marketing).

A common way to drive revenue through email marketing is doing lifecycle campaigns aimed at upselling customers. As an example, WP Engine, a WordPress hosting company, uses lifecycle campaigns to get users on one of their premium plans.

They've built a WordPress blog speed tester tool (at speed.wpengine. com) where interested prospects can enter their site URL and email address to get a free report about their site's performance.

Over the course of a month, WP Engine will then send that prospect an email course about WordPress speed and scalability – three quick ways to improve your site speed, why hosting is important for business, etc. Near the end of this mini-course, WP Engine will make a pitch to sign up for their premium WordPress hosting service.

This seven-email sequence leads to a better conversion rate than driving potential users to a sales landing page. In fact, many companies like WP Engine now use advertising to drive leads to a landing page where they ask for an email rather than a sale. They then will use email to sell a prospect over the course of a month or so.

When WP Engine has prospects they know are not ready to convert, they put them on a different list where they send them (less frequent) monthly emails with relevant content. When it later comes time for these prospects to go looking for premium WordPress hosting, you can guess where they go.

Email retargeting is another tool you can use for revenue. For example, if one of your users abandoned a shopping cart, send them a targeted email a day or two later with a special offer for whatever item they left in the cart. Targeted emails will always convert better than an email asking for a sale out of the blue.

For feature-based freemium products, emails that explain a premium feature a customer is missing out on can have high conversion rate. For example, if you ran a dating website, you could explain that upgrading to a premium plan will lead to more dates. If you have a subscription product, ask them to upgrade to annual billing, which guarantees they will not cancel within the next year.

Similarly, if you run a scaled pricing business (e.g. you pay $9/month for 5 users, $20/month for 10 users, and so on), you can set up special emails for users nearing their plan limits and ask them to upgrade. For example, when you're about to run out of Skype credits, Skype will email you asking you to re-up or upgrade to a subscription service.

## Email Marketing for Referrals

Due to the personal nature of email, it is excellent for generating customer referrals. If a friend emails you to tell you about a new product they are enjoying, you're far more likely to try it than if you saw them mention it briefly on Facebook.

Groupon generates referrals by giving users an incentive to tell their friends about discounts. Unless a certain number of people have purchased a Groupon, the discount is not valid. Thus, as someone who wants 50% off their meal at Cheesecake Factory, we will happily email our friends so the deal happens.

This kind of referral program was a major growth driver for Dropbox as well. In order to get more free space, users send referral emails asking their friends to check out Dropbox. If a friend signs up, both users get extra free space. This referral program (built on top of email referrals) has been Dropbox's biggest growth mechanism and has led to tens of millions of users.

Some consumer apps, and even some B2B companies like Asana, will ask their users to import their address books to share the site with their friends. This marketing tactic touches elements of both viral and email marketing and can be extremely effective. In fact, many of the viral products you know of (Hotmail, Facebook, LinkedIn) grew by cleverly using email marketing.

## Tactics

Deliverability is a key factor in email. For many technical reasons, your email messages may not be reaching their intended recipients. Most companies use an email-marketing provider like MailChimp or Constant Contact to send their emails. These companies help ensure deliverability, which can be quite complicated.

As with other traction channels, testing is essential to maximize this channel's impact. Effective email campaigns A/B test every aspect: subjects, formats, images, timing and more.

Timing is especially relevant to get higher open rates: many marketers suggest sending emails between 9 a.m.–12 p.m. in your customer's time zone or scheduling emails to reach them at the time they registered for your email list (e.g. for users who signed up for your list at 8 p.m., email them at 8 p.m.). This is another variable you should test yourself, as its efficacy varies depending on the product.

One of email's strengths is that it's a way to get feedback from your customers. One trick Colin told us about was not to send any email that comes from a "Noreply" email address (e.g. noreply@facebook. com). Instead, use that opportunity to send the automated email from a personal address and allow the recipient to reply with questions or problems they have. This can be great for support, feature requests and for selling existing customers.

Lastly, an effective lifecycle sequence will be meaningless if you don't have great email copy. Copywriting is an art on its own, but we suggest checking out some of the resources and information that Copyhackers provides. An email campaign can easily go from a waste of time to wildly profitable just by tweaking a few words and headlines.

## Takeaways

- Email marketing is a personal traction channel. Messages come into your inbox along with email from your friends and family. As such, the more personalized your email marketing messages, the better they perform.

- You can utilize email marketing at any step of your relationship with a customer, including customer acquisition, activation, retention, and revenue generation.

- We recommend building an email list of potential customers whether you end up focusing on this traction channel or not.

- A particularly effective email marketing technique is to set up a series of automated emails (often called lifecycle or drip sequences) to send to customers or prospective customers. This technique works best when this series of emails adapts to how people have interacted with your product and asks them to take specific actions at some point.

- We recommend using online tools to ensure reliable delivery and to help you test and optimize email campaigns.

See our email marketing resources and discuss this traction channel with us and other startup founders on our forum:

http://tbook.us/email

# CHAPTER 15

# Engineering as Marketing

Your team's engineering skills can get your startup traction directly by building tools and resources that reach more people. We call this traction channel engineering as marketing. You make useful tools like calculators, widgets, and educational micro-sites to get your company in front of potential customers. These tools generate leads and expand your customer base.

In this chapter we present examples of companies like HubSpot and RJ Metrics that have successfully used this under-utilized channel for rapid growth.

## *Effective Engineering as Marketing*

HubSpot, a marketing automation software company, has reached tens of millions in revenue in a few short years. One key to their success is a free marketing review tool they created called Marketing Grader.

When you enter your site's web address into Marketing Grader, you get back a customized report about how well you're doing with your online marketing (social media mentions, blog post shares, basic SEO). This tool is free and gives you valuable information. It also provides HubSpot with information they use to qualify you as a potential prospect. After all, someone who wants to evaluate the success of their site's marketing is a good candidate for HubSpot's marketing tool. These are quality leads!

We spoke with HubSpot's founder, Dharmesh Shah, about Marketing Grader (formerly called Website Grader). His story gave us insight on where ideas for engineering as marketing tools come from:

*"The early story of Website Grader is interesting. There were only three people at HubSpot at the time. My co-founder and I would regularly "sell" (in the early days, a lot of those sales calls were with friends, and friends of friends). One of the initial steps in the sales process was for me to get a sense for how good a given company's website was at inbound marketing. My co-founder (Brian Halligan) would constantly send me websites he wanted me to take a look at so we could determine if they were a good fit.*

*After a few days of this, I got tired of going through the manual steps (look at Alexa, look at their page titles, check out their domain, etc.). So, I built an application to automate that process for me. On a related note, I had also started angel investing at the time, and I used the same process to assess the marketing savviness of potential startups I was considering investing in. Once the app was built (it didn't take more than a few days for the initial version), I thought it might be useful for other people, so I registered "websitegrader.com" and made the app available publicly. We eventually started collecting email addresses in the app, and kept iterating on it."*

Since HubSpot launched Marketing Grader, over three million sites have used it. Dharmesh said that it accounts for a large portion of the 50,000+ leads HubSpot gets each month.

Marketing Grader is so powerful for Hubspot because it precisely serves the needs of their target audience. It's a low-friction way to draw leads into the HubSpot sales funnel. Engineering as marketing is particularly effective for HubSpot because Marketing Grader complements their primary product so well.

Another company that nails engineering as marketing is Moz, the leader in SEO software. Two of their free SEO tools, Followerwonk and Open Site Explorer, have driven tens of thousands of leads for Moz. Like Marketing Grader, each solves a problem that an ideal Moz customer has. Followerwonk allows users to analyze their Twitter followers and get tips on growing their audience. Open Site Explorer allows users to see where sites are getting links, which is valuable competitive intelligence for any SEO campaign.

A key feature of these tools is their ease of use: prospects simply go to the site and enter a domain name or Twitter handle. Once someone uses the tools, companies can begin to engage these potential customers through other traction channels like sales and email marketing.

## Converting Potential Customers

WP Engine, a WordPress hosting provider, is another prime example of a company using this channel successfully. The hosting market is saturated with hundreds of hosting companies, yet WP Engine has cornered the market on high-end WordPress hosting. This is thanks in part to their free tool that checks how fast your WordPress site loads.

The WP Engine speed testing tool asks for only an email address in exchange for a detailed report about your site's speed. It also gives you the option to opt in for a free mini-course about improving the speed of your blog. Once they have a user's email, they send them tips about improving their site speed and end with a sales pitch, as described in the email marketing chapter.

Dharmesh mentioned that it helps him to think of these tools as marketing *assets* with ongoing returns, rather than ads that result in a one-time boost.

*"I think of free tools as content (albeit, interactive content). At HubSpot, we really believe in marketing channels that have high leverage (i.e. write it or build it once – and get value forever). As such, we take a very geeky*

*and analytical approach to marketing. We think of each piece of content (blog article, app, video, whatever) as a marketing asset. This asset creates a return – often indefinitely.*

*We contrast that to buying an ad which does not scale as well. When you advertise, the money you're spending is what drives how much attention you get. Want more clicks? Spend more money. Contrast this to inbound marketing whereby the cost of producing a piece of content is relatively constant. But, if it generates 10x more leads in a month, your marginal cost for those extra leads is almost zero. Further, with advertising (outbound marketing), the traffic you get generally stops when you stop paying. With inbound marketing, even \*after\* you stop producing new content, the old content can still drive ongoing visitors and leads."*

The case for spending engineering resources on marketing becomes much stronger when you think about the resulting tools as assets. These tools have the potential to become a continual source of leads that make up the majority of your traction.

## Tactics

### Annual Promotions

One way  to boost your efforts in this traction channel is to take advantage of cyclical behavior. Take Codecademy's Code Year micro-site, which launched at the beginning of 2012. Many people claim to want to learn how to code, but don't follow through. Code Year addressed that issue by asking users to enter their email address to receive a free lesson about programming each week during 2012. Over 450,000 individuals signed up on CodeYear.com, nearly doubling Codecademy's userbase at the time.

Similarly, Patrick McKenzie from Bingo Card Creator makes holiday themed micro-sites for Halloween, Christmas, and other holidays. These sites remain relevant for far longer than you might expect.

Since they are tied to the holidays, Bingo Card Creator can use them year after year. In Codecademy's case, you could actually sign up for Code Year at any point during the year and still receive a weekly lesson.

### Micro-Sites

When Gabriel (co-author) wrote blog posts about search privacy, he got a big response from readers. After engaging with commenters in social media channels it became clear that this is a topic that really resonated with people. Gabriel had the idea that a micro-site might address people's concerns more fully while simultaneously exposing his search engine, DuckDuckGo, to a broader audience.

In 2011, Gabriel built such a micro-site, DontTrack.us, which showed how Google tracks your searches and why that can harm you. The site raised awareness about these practices and spread virally. At the same time, readers learned that DuckDuckGo does not track users or store their personal information.

Even after the initial wave of press and users, this micro-site has been useful. As unpredictable events unfold (like news of NSA tracking) or predictable events reoccur (like Data Privacy Day), the traffic on the ever-present micro-site persists. Users of DuckDuckGo often send the site to friends and family to explain the issues surrounding search tracking. The strategy worked so well that DuckDuckGo now has four micro-sites and is planning more.

One tactic to really maximize impact is to put your tools on their own website. This simple technique does two things. First, it makes them much easier to share. Second, you can do well with SEO by picking a name that people search often so your tool is more naturally discoverable (see chapter 12).

### Widgets

Chris Fralic (former Head of business development at Delicious and Half.com) tells us that creating a Delicious bookmark widget more than tripled the adoption of their social bookmarking product.

How many times have you seen Facebook, Twitter and other sharing buttons on a site? For each of those widgets (e.g. Facebook, Stumble-Upon, Google+, and Twitter buttons), a company used engineering resources to create a marketing tool that was embeddable on sites. These widgets drive engagement, traffic and traction for these social platforms and the sites that use these tools.

## Case Study: RJMetrics

We also spoke with Robert Moore, founder of RJMetrics (an ecommerce Analytics company) to learn how they've used this traction channel to drive the majority of their leads and sales. As an engineer himself, Robert said he's been using his engineering skills to bring in customers since he founded the company.

For example, they use their own product to discover interesting trends on some of the most popular social media sites like Twitter, Tumblr, Instagram and Pinterest. A recent post was entitled "BuzzFeed Posts: What's the Magic Number for 'Best Of' Lists?"

These posts gave them big traffic spikes when they launched, and led to a lot of long-tail opportunities as people discovered the content over time. Robert mentioned that they've been approached multiple times by writers for major publications who want to cite them as a source. OK Cupid, a dating site, has a similar strategy that we covered under content marketing (Chapter 13).

Though their engineering efforts have certainly helped their content marketing, RJ Metrics seriously began to use this channel when they started building tools and micro-sites. They own (and create content for) domains like cohortanalysis.com and querymongo.com, which contain keywords a potential RJ Metrics customer would search for.

In the case of querymongo.com, they built a tool that translates SQL queries to MongoDB syntax (two database technologies). This is useful for developers or product managers starting to use MongoDB but who are still more familiar with SQL. It also drives leads for RJ Metrics, because anyone doing data analysis is a potential customer for their main product. Querymongo is RJ's highest-trafficked micro-site and drives hundreds of leads per month.

Robert said they look for high ROI on engineering time: if a few days of engineering time can drive hundreds of leads, that's an investment they make whenever they can.

## Conclusion

Engineering as marketing creates lasting assets that can serve as the engine for your growth. Zack Linford, the founder of Optimozo and Conversion Voodoo, talked about how building tools can help with PR and SEO, while also nailing down the core value proposition for your product. As he mentioned in our interview:

*"Building noteworthy tools that your target audience finds useful is a solid way to gain traction that also pays dividends down the road by helping build your SEO. A simple roadmap to executing this technical strategy includes:*

- *Providing something of true value for free, with no strings attached.*

- *Making that offering extremely relevant to your core business.*

- *Demonstrating that value as quickly as possible."*

When you build valuable tools for prospective customers, you get more leads, a stronger brand, and increased awareness while also solving a problem for the individuals you want to target.

Dharmesh mentioned that engineering as marketing is especially valuable because so few companies use it:

*"I'm a big believer in using an engineering approach to marketing. But, I'm biased (being an engineer myself). And yes, there are many other*

*marketing channels available, but creating applications has a unique investment/return profile. Since it is considerably harder to build a very popular application, fewer people do it: so, the "free apps" channel is usually less saturated.*

*The best companies to use this apps-powered model are software companies. In this case, they can launch complementary apps – or subsets – for free. This not only creates value that draws people in, it also educates people on what the main product does."*

Companies have a hard time using engineering resources for anything but product development. Any technical focus on something other than product seems wasted since engineering time is so expensive. As a result, most founders and product managers use all their engineering resources to build new features for a product that's struggling to acquire users. Don't make the same mistake. Instead, consider using some of that engineering time to build a tool that moves the needle for your business.

## Takeaways

- The goal of engineering as marketing should be creating a low-friction way to engage potential customers that naturally leads to your main offering.

- A cheap test for this traction channel is to develop and push out a small tool or site. Perhaps you have already started creating one for yourself that could also be used by potential customers? Another approach is to turn a popular blog post into a micro-site.

- A great way to keep tools low-friction is to make them as simple as possible. Single-purpose tools that solve obvious pain points are best. Put them on their own website and make them easy to find, particularly through search engines.

- The case for spending engineering resources on marketing becomes much stronger when you think about these marketing tools as long-term assets that bring in new leads indefinitely after only a small amount of upfront investment.

See our engineering as marketing resources and discuss this traction channel with us and other startup founders on our forum:

http://tbook.us/eam

# CHAPTER 16

# Targeting Blogs

Targeting blogs your customers read is one of the most effective ways to get your first wave of customers. However, this traction channel can be difficult to scale in phase II and III due to the limited number of relevant high-traffic blogs. That's ok. Not all traction channels are infinitely scalable. In fact, using tactics that don't scale is one of the best ways to get your first users. Paul Graham put it like this:

*"The need to do something unscalably laborious to get started is so nearly universal that it might be a good idea to stop thinking of startup ideas as scalars. Instead we should try thinking of them as pairs of what you're going to build, plus the unscalable thing(s) you're going to do initially to get the company going."*

We interviewed Noah Kagan, former head of marketing at Mint and founder of AppSumo, to learn how he used this channel to acquire more than 20,000 users before Mint's launch.

## Finding Blogs

It can be difficult to uncover the smaller blogs that cover your niche. Here are several tools you can use to find all the influential bloggers in your space:

**Search Engines** – Simply search for things like "top blogs for x" or "best x blogs."

**YouTube** – Doing a simple search for your product keywords on YouTube shows you the most popular videos in your industry. These videos are often associated with influencers that have blogs, and you use references to their videos as an icebreaker to start building a relationship with them. This tactic can be applied to other video sharing sites, such as Vimeo and Dailymotion.

**Delicious** – Delicious allows you to use keywords to find links that others have saved, which can unearth new blogs.

**Twitter** – Using Twitter search is another easy way to find blogs in a niche. You can also use tools like Followerwonk and Klout to determine the top Twitter accounts in your industry.

**Social Mention** – Social Mention helps you determine the sites that have the most frequent mentions for your keywords..

**Talk to people** – The most effective way to figure out what your target audience is really reading online is by asking directly!

## Case Study: Mint

Mint's story is impressive. They launched their simple money management site in 2007, and – less than two years later – Intuit acquired them for $170 million. In between, Mint was able to acquire over 1.5 million users, 20,000 of whom signed up *before* they even launched. Within six months of Mint's launch, they had over one million users.

Very few startups experience this kind of growth during their first six months. Noah Kagan, founder of AppSumo and Mint's director of marketing, drove many of their early marketing efforts. As he told us in our interview, Mint's phase I goal was to get 100,000 users within six months.

To hit those numbers, Noah created a quant-based marketing spreadsheet like this:

| Source | Traffic | CTR | Conversion % | Total Users | Status | Confirmed | Confirmed Users |
|---|---|---|---|---|---|---|---|
| TechCrunch | 300000 | 10% | 25% | 7500 | Friend | Yes | 7500 |
| Dave McClure | 30000 | 10% | 25% | 750 | Friend | Yes | 750 |
| Mashable | 500000 | 10% | 25% | 12500 | Emailing | No | 0 |
| Reddit | 25000 | 100% | 25% | 6250 | Coordinated | Yes | 6250 |
| Digg | 100000 | 100% | 25% | 25000 | Coordinated | Yes | 25000 |
| Google Organic | 5000 | 100% | 15% | 750 | Receiving | Yes | 750 |
| Google Ads | 1000000 | 3% | 35% | 10500 | Bought | Yes | 10500 |
| Paul Stamatiou | 50000 | 5% | 50% | 1250 | Friend | Yes | 1250 |
| Personal Finance Sponsorships | 200000 | 40% | 65% | 52000 | Coordinated | Yes | 52000 |
| Okdork.com | 3000 | 10% | 75% | 225 | Self | Yes | 225 |
| | | | | | | | |
| Total Users | | | | 116725 | | | 104225 |

His spreadsheet listed traction channels Mint planned to mine for potential users. Then, Noah ran the numbers in terms of traffic, click-through rates (CTR), and conversions (actually signing up for their product in this case), and calculated the number of expected users from each channel strategy.

Next, he confirmed the channels Mint would focus on by running tests that seemed promising. To test blogs, he contacted a few that were representative of different customer segments, and got them to write articles about Mint. This method is a version of the Bullseye Framework we presented in the introduction: he systematically set out to determine which channel would allow him to accomplish his specific traction goal.

This series of tests revealed that targeting blogs was the channel to focus on since they were getting great conversion rates and they could reach enough people to attain their goal. Noah then created a long list of blogs to target, and set about contacting those blogs about guest posts, coverage, and placing Mint badges on their sites. Through this focusing process, Noah uncovered tactics that further improved their traction through this channel: VIP access and sponsoring.

**VIP Access**

Mint did something that few startups had done before them to increase awareness and build excitement for their launch: they asked people on their pre-launch waiting list to recommend Mint to their friends in return for priority product access.

As part of the signup process, users could embed an "I want Mint" badge on their personal blogs, Facebook, or other websites. Users that drove signups through these badges were rewarded with VIP access before other invites were sent out.

The key to the success of these badges was to make them easy to share and embed. Much like YouTube provides an embed code below each video on their site, Mint provided the code necessary to make embedding badges as simple as copying and pasting. Many users were happy to place the small badge on their website in order to get early access to a product they wanted. Mint had 600 blogs display the badge and 50,000 users signed up through them. This tactic also gave Mint an SEO boost from the hundreds of new links pointing to mint.com.

**Sponsoring**

Mint used a second innovative tactic to acquire users through this channel: sponsoring blogs. Each sponsored blog would put a small Mint advertisement on their site for a period of time. Noah tracked each advertisement to see which blogs were most effective and how many people signed up. Not only did this approach contribute over 10,000 pre-registrations for the product, but it also allowed the Mint team to understand the kind of user most interested in their product.

Many personal bloggers have strong readerships but don't make money from their writing. Noah offered them a way to show off a cool new service and make some money doing it. Noah simply sent them a message with "Can I send you $500?" as the subject and told them a bit about the product and what Mint was trying to do. Most were happy to share a useful product with their audiences and make some money in the process.

Mint also created content partnerships with larger sites like The Motley Fool, a personal investing site. With this content partnership (each site contributed content to the other), Mint exposed their valuable, free product to over three million readers who would likely be interested in their service. This post-launch content partnership combined targeting blogs with elements of business development (see chapter 17) and was a big win for the Mint team.

Noah used this traction channel again at AppSumo, his startup that sells software bundles and educational products at discounted prices. To get traction, Noah pulled together free bundles for blogs and conferences, such as SXSW.

One of the first bundles AppSumo did was specifically for Lifehacker, a popular productivity blog. Rather than just trying to pitch Lifehacker on his new startup, Noah built a product bundle for them before reaching out. Lifehacker couldn't turn down a bundle geared specifically towards their users. In their words:

*"Our love of free software here at Lifehacker is no secret, but sometimes you just need to shell out for some advanced features. AppSumo is currently offering a bundle of our favorite productivity webapps, for a fraction of the price."*

The offer did really well with Lifehacker's audience, and led to strong early traction for AppSumo. Noah also sponsored blogs to run AppSumo giveaways, much like he did at Mint. AppSumo is now a profitable business with over 800,000 customers.

## Link-Sharing Communities

Sharing links is at the heart of many large communities on the web (e.g. reddit, Hacker News, Inbound.org and Digg). In addition, there are hundreds of niche communities and forums that encourage and reward the sharing of links.

Dropbox, the file storage startup, targeted these communities for their initial traction. By sharing a video on Hacker News, Dropbox received over 10,000 signups. Soon, they were trending on Digg (significantly bigger at the time), which drove even more signups.

Quora, reddit, Codecademy, and Gumroad saw similar success from initial postings on Hacker News because their products were a good fit for users of that site. The founders behind Filepicker.io – a file management tool for developers – also posted a basic demo there, looking for some feedback and early users. Their submission was in the top spot on for nearly three hours, during which they saw:

- 10,000+ visits in 4 hours

- 460 concurrent users

- 12,000+ people using the demo over the course of the day

- 500+ developer sign-ups

- 5,000+ files managed

## Conclusion

As we saw with Mint and others, targeting blogs is a great way to get your first wave of users. In a crowded online environment, reaching prospects in an arena where they choose to spend time is a valuable way to get traction.

## Takeaways

- Targeting blogs is one of the most effective ways to get your first wave of customers.

- There are a variety of tools you can use to uncover relevant blogs including YouTube, Delicious, StumbleUpon, Twitter, search engines, Google Alerts and Social Mention.

- You can run tests on a variety of smaller blogs to see what type of blog and blog audience resonates best with your product and messaging.

- Small blog sponsorships (especially to personal blogs) can be an effective tactic. Another is providing influential bloggers early access or offering early access in exchange for spreading the word.

- When launching, link-sharing communities can be an effective tool to generate traffic, feedback, and buzz.

See our targeting blogs resources and discuss this traction channel with us and other startup founders on our forum:

http://tbook.us/blogs

# CHAPTER 17

# Business Development (BD)

Business development is like sales with one key distinction: it is primarily focused on exchanging value through partnerships, whereas sales primarily focuses on exchanging dollars for a product.

With sales, you're selling directly to a customer. With business development, you're partnering to reach customers in a way that benefits both parties.

We interviewed Chris Fralic, former senior business development executive at AOL, Half.com, eBay, and Delicious, and current partner at First Round Capital. Chris described how he used business development successfully at each of his startups (all of which were acquired).

Many companies like Delicious got traction through business development. Even Google, a company whose early success is often attributed to only a superior product, got most of their initial traction from two key partnerships. In 1999, they partnered with Netscape to be their default search engine for the popular Netscape Navigator web browser. Google also reached an agreement with Yahoo!, then (and still) one of the largest web properties in existence, to power their online searches. These two deals were critical to Google's eventual success as the world's largest search engine.

## Types of Partnerships

Here are the major types of business development partnerships:

### Standard Partnerships

In a standard partnership, two companies work together to make one or both of their products better by leveraging the unique capabilities of the other. One prominent example is the Apple/Nike partnership that resulted in the Nike+ shoe that communicates with your iPod or iPhone to track your runs and play music.

### Joint Ventures

In a joint venture, two companies work together to create an entirely new product offering. These types of deals are complex and often require large investments, long periods of time, and (sometimes) equity exchanges. If you've ever bought a bottled Starbucks Frappuccino or Doubleshot Espresso, you've purchased a product that's the result of the decade-long joint venture between Starbucks and Pepsi.

### Licensing

Licensing works well when one company has a strong brand an upstart wants to use in a new product or service. To use another Starbucks example, they lent their brand to an ice cream manufacturer that wanted to create Starbucks-flavored ice cream. Other startups, like Spotify and Grooveshark, are forced into licensing agreements by nature of their business. They can't use music content without first licensing it from the record labels that own it.

### Distribution Deals

In these deals, one party provides a product or service to the other in return for access to potential customers. Groupon's core business is structured like this: they work with a restaurant or store to offer a discount to Groupon's mailing list. Paul English, founder of Kayak, told us how an early distribution deal with AOL was responsible for Kayak's early traction.

Through this partnership, Kayak used their search technology to power an AOL-owned travel search engine, which drove a lot of traffic right out of the gate.

**Supply Partners**

These types of partnerships help you secure key inputs which are essential for certain products. As we'll see, Half.com formed several to ensure they had enough books to sell when they launched their online bookstore. Other supply partnerships include Youtube's relationships with channel partners and deals between suppliers and companies like Wal-Mart.

## Strategic Business Development

Business development can drive some amazing outcomes for your startup. However, getting traction from this channel requires something that few companies do well: strategic thinking.

For business development to work, you must have a clear understanding of your company objectives. What metrics do you need to hit in order to maximize your chances of success? How can partnerships help you get there? **Good BD deals align with your company and product strategy and are focused on critical product and distribution milestones.** These deals should help you hit your key metrics, whether growth, revenue, or product-related.

At Half.com, they identified three key things needed to succeed: technology, inventory, and distribution. With these in mind, Chris formed strategic partnerships to increase their chances of success.

*"In the case of Half.com, there were three key things that we needed before we launched. Number one, the site had to work. We needed technology partners (back in the pre-Amazon cloud days) to ensure people could actually use the site.*

*Then there was inventory. We decided we needed one million books, movies, etc. at launch because that sounded like a nice big number. So my team and I worked on how we get product on the shelves. It was our job (prior to launch) to find inventory and get it listed on the site.*

*The third was to get distribution. We went out and created one of the early affiliate programs and did distribution and marketing partnerships."*

Thanks to their business development efforts, Half.com had a network of partners around the time of their launch that looked like this:

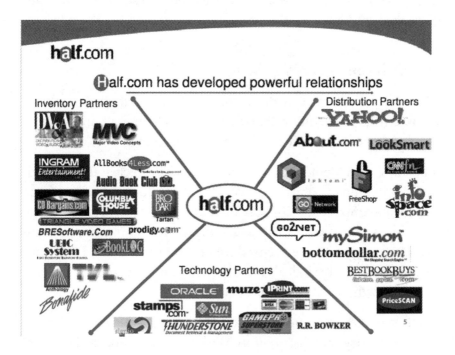

Once their objectives were identified, Chris and his team were able to form partnerships that allowed them to launch with one of the largest selections of books and movies anywhere at the time.

## Picking the Right Partners

Understanding a partner's goals is key to creating a mutually beneficial relationship. Chris mentioned that startups are often focused on themselves and their needs without considering why a potential partner should make the deal:

*"It's research and learning and understanding your partner's business before you start picking up the phone or sending emails. You need to understand what's on their side of the table – what are their issues?*

*To pick one example, we wanted to find books that were half off and find big quantities of inventory. So I started doing research to find big piles of used inventory and literally started calling people, asking people questions to understand how their business worked. We found out how products moved from book publishers out to the Borders of the world, where it came back to and where it accumulated when it didn't sell. Once we found out where, we ended up getting partnerships with those people. I even flew to Atlanta and literally worked in a used bookstore for a day."*

You need to understand *why* a potential partner should want to work with you. What are their incentives? **Just as you evaluate potential partnerships in terms of your core metrics, they will be doing the same.** You should also seek out forward-thinking partners. Often that means finding an advocate inside a large company or working with a company that has done deals with startups in the past.

At First Round Capital, Chris now works with entrepreneurs to determine how they can use business development at their companies. He asks specifically: "what do you want your fundraising deck to look like in 12 months?" Answering this question helps founders think through key milestones they need to reach, and then work backwards to think about partnerships or distribution arrangements that could help them get there.

## Creating a BD Pipeline

Not every partnership will end up working. Thus, **it makes sense to build a pipeline of deals**. Charlie O'Donnell, partner at VC firm Brooklyn Bridge Ventures, suggests maintaining a large list of potential partners:

*"Create an exhaustive list of all of your possible [partners]. Don't ever list Condé Nast without listing every single other publisher you can think of. Make a very simple spreadsheet: Company, Partner Type (Publisher, Carrier, Reseller, etc.), Contact person/email, Size, Relevance, Ease of Use, and then a subjective priority score. That list should be \*exhaustive\*.*

*There's no reason why any company shouldn't have 50 potential business development partners in their pipeline, maybe 100, and be actively working the phones, inboxes, and pounding the pavement to get the deals you need to get – be it for distribution, revenue, PR, or just to outflank a competitor. The latter is totally underutilized. If you go in and impress the top 50 folks in your space, it makes it that much harder for a competitor to get a deal done – because you're seen as the category leader."*

Once you have a list of potential partners, send it to your investors, friends, and advisors for warm introductions.

Chris Fralic suggests putting potential partners into buckets based on attributes. For example, you might categorize based on revenue numbers, distribution reach, or inventory capabilities. Then, at the end of this process, choose 10–20 partners to focus your business development efforts on. As he said:

*"People tend to get caught up on the names – 'is this a known name' – and place more emphasis on that than what might be more important elements. So I'd encourage people to think about the attributes of your partner. So rather than saying 'I want to go after XYZ brand', say 'we want to go after Internet retailers that are between 50 and 250 on the IR [Internet Retailer] 500 – because that puts them in this kind of revenue range – and have a director of ecommerce.'"*

Chris pitched all kinds of deals during his time at Delicious, the social bookmarking site. While he was there, he worked on deals with *The Washington Post*, Mozilla, and Wikipedia to integrate Delicious tags.

Delicious approached their potential partners with a clear idea of how each of them would benefit from a partnership.

For *The Washington Post*, the value proposition was clear: use Delicious' social bookmarks to optimize content for social media. *The Washington Post's* decision to partner was made even easier because it was a simple integration with very little downside. After integrating with *The Washington Post*, the number of sites interested in a Delicious extension skyrocketed because of the *Post's* role as a media leader. It even made other partnerships, like the browser integration with Mozilla's Firefox, possible:

*"The even more transformative partnership we did at Delicious was with Mozilla. [Mozilla] ended up promoting the Delicious extension for the Firefox browser in a really big way when they did an upgrade to Firefox 2.0. The net of it was that when huge portions of their audience were upgrading, one of the first things they saw was the Delicious extension. It ultimately more than tripled our userbase, just from that partnership."*

Chris stressed that **you can be assured that not every deal will close; in fact, most deals won't.** For example, Delicious pursued an integration deal with Wikipedia that failed. Delicious was able to get traction from business development because they developed a large pipeline of potential deals.

## *The BD Process*

Once you have a few partners you're targeting, the real action starts. You start approaching potential partners with a value-focused proposition that outlines why they should work with you. Often these are larger companies. Brenda Spoonemore, former Senior VP of Interactive Services at the NBA, put it like this:

*"What do you have that they (big companies) need? You're more focused than they are. You have an idea and you're solving a problem. You've developed content or technology and you have a focus. That is very difficult to do at a big corporation."*

To approach these deals, you want to first identify the right contact at your target company. Some companies will have a business development department that handles partnerships, but – depending on the deal – it could be someone like a product director or C-level executive you want to engage with.

Once identified, you want to try to get a warm introduction to that person. With each introduction, you should provide the mutual contact with an overview of your proposal that can easily be forwarded. Then, be sure to follow up and set timelines for next steps. Chris mentioned that it was key for him to get a meeting or phone call set up as quickly as possible – sometimes even on the same day.

After the proposal stage comes a negotiation of a terms sheet. The key terms will usually be the lifetime of the deal, exclusivity, how payments work (if any), the level of commitment between partners, any guarantees in the deal, and revenue sharing agreements.

Both Chris and Brenda suggest making the negotiation and term sheet as simple as possible – often just one page. The simpler you can make it to work together (and the fewer lawyers that need to get involved), the easier partnering will be.

Keeping it simple is especially good advice for technology partnerships. With engineering time so valuable, do as much as you can to make it easy for potential partners to work with you. For example, Delicious built *The Washington Post* a custom interface for their readers to post bookmarks. Rather than involving the *Post's* IT resources, Delicious made it easy to them set up and going.

Once a deal is completed, obviously you want to maintain a positive relationship with the new partner. It's also important to understand the driving factors that got the deal accomplished.

Chris suggests making a "how the deal was done" memo documenting how long it took to get to milestones, key contacts, sticking points, what interested the prospect enough to become a partner and other factors that influenced the completion of the deal. These memos help companies determine what's working in their process and what could be improved upon.

## Business Development 2.0

Business development has historically been a high-touch process that includes a lot of personal interactions. Reaching out to partners, understanding their needs, and negotiating terms are all part of a traditional business deal. However, businesses recently have been moving to more low-touch business development. Low-touch BD utilizes tools like APIs, feeds, crawling technology and embed codes to reach new distribution channels and grow your influence. These methods allow you to standardize your value proposition and get more deals done.

Nevertheless, it still makes sense to land a few traditional deals first, and then transition to low-touch partnerships. Delicious's first key partnerships with Mozilla and *The Washington Post* happened in the traditional way. These partnerships generated significant traction for Delicious, so they made their API publicly available to the many sites that wanted to integrate with them. This required some up-front engineering work, but also meant that Delicious could now integrate with thousands of sites interested in leveraging their product.

Other companies have pursued low-touch business development in a similar way. SlideShare makes all slideshows embeddable, Disqus has their easy comment system installation, and SoundCloud makes their music library freely accessible. Such integrations fuel growth and vastly increase the pool of potential partners for a company.

However, just building a great API does not mean people will come and use it. Landing those first few partners through traditional means ensures that someone is getting value from working with your startup. Later, once you have more demand, you can start to standardize and simplify the partnership and integration process.

## Conclusion

Whether you are starting out or scaling to millions of users, business development can move the needle in any product phase. Kayak is a perfect example of this. As we mentioned, they got their first users through a key partnership with AOL. Later, they partnered with hotel chains, rental agencies, and other groups to extend their reach to new groups of customers. The right deal at the right time can propel your company to the next phase of growth.

## Takeaways

- Business development is the pursuit of mutually beneficial partnerships. In a standard partnership, two companies work together to make one or both of their products better by leveraging the unique capabilities of the other.

- Other major types of BD deals include partnerships focused on joint ventures, licensing, distribution, and inventory.

- Good business development deals align with your company and product strategy and are focused on strategic product and distribution milestones. These deals should focus on meeting your startup's core metrics, whether they be growth, revenue or something else.

- You need to understand why a potential partner might want to work with you. What are their incentives? Just as you are evaluating potential partnerships in terms of your core metrics, they will be doing the same.

- Most deals fail, which is why it is critical to create a constant pipeline of deals. For initial testing, you can reach out to a variety of potential partners to gauge initial interest.

See our business development resources and discuss this traction channel with us and other startup founders on our forum:

http://tbook.us/bd

# CHAPTER 18

# Sales

Sales is the process of generating leads, qualifying them, and converting them into paying customers. This channel is particularly useful for products that require interpersonal interaction before a purchase (often enterprise and expensive ones). That's because hand-holding prospects can be necessary to turn prospects into real customers. One effective way to do that is via sales.

Scaling this traction channel requires you to design and implement a repeatable sales model. We also cover how to get those first few customers, build your sales funnel, and tactics you can use in common sales situations like cold calling.

**Closing First Customers**
For consumer products, your first customers will likely come through channels other than sales – SEO, SEM, targeting blogs and the like. When targeting bigger businesses, however, closing those first few critical customers can be significantly more challenging.

**Early Conversations**
We interviewed Sean Murphy, owner of customer development and sales consulting firm SKMurphy, to talk about how he helps startups get their first enterprise customers:

*"Most of the time [their first customer] is going to be somebody they know or we know. For the most part, our clients are going into a market that they understand with technology that they have developed.*

*We help them make a list of every project they've worked on and every-*

*one they've worked with. They reach out and say, 'Here is what we are doing: do you know somebody we should talk to that makes sense?'*

*People who've developed expertise by working in a field for a while are typically able to get an initial meeting – cup of coffee or lunch, these kinds of things. Sometimes we encourage them to shift to a different market because we find out that the technology has more applicability and offers more value there. One of the first things we help them with is what we call a lunch pitch. This is a single piece of paper that has five to ten bullets and a perhaps a visual that helps them focus the conversation making sure they understand the prospect's problem. The early conversations are all about exploring the prospect's problem and pain points."*

Talking to prospects about their problems is not only a necessary sales tactic, but also a product development one. John Raguin, co-founder of insurance software company Guidewire Software, explained their approach to reaching their first prospective customers:

*"We went to our potential customers, insurance companies, and proposed to do a short free consulting study that would provide [an assessment] of their operation. We would spend approximately 7–10 man-days of effort understanding their operations, and at the end we would give them a high-level presentation benchmarking them as compared to their peers. In return, we asked for feedback on what would make the best system that would meet their needs. In the end, we were able to work with over 40 insurance companies this way. We were honest about our motives at all times, and we made sure to provide quality output."*

When it comes to structuring your sales conversations, we suggest using the approach developed by Neil Rackham as outlined in his book, *SPIN Selling.* It is a four-part question framework to use when talking to prospects, based on a decade spent researching 35,000 sales calls:

1. **Situation questions.** These questions help you learn about a prospect's buying situation. Typical questions may include *'How many employees do you have?'* and *'How is your organization structured?'*

2. Only ask one or two of these questions per conversation since the more situation questions a salesperson asks the less likely they are to close a sale. That's because people feel like they're giving you information without getting anything in return. This is especially true of executive decision-makers who are likely more pressed for time. Make sure you ask just enough situation questions to determine if you're talking to a likely candidate for a sale.

3. **Problem questions.** These are questions that clarify the buyer's pain points. *Are you happy with your current solution? What problems do you face with it?*

   Like situation questions, these questions should be used sparingly. You want to quickly define the problem they're facing so you can focus on the implications of this problem and how your solution helps.

4. **Implication questions**. These questions are meant to make a prospect aware of the implications that stem from the problem they're facing. These questions are based on information you uncovered while asking your problem questions. Questions could include –

   *Does this problem hurt your productivity? How many people does this issue impact, and in what ways? What customer or employee turnover are you experiencing because of this problem?*

   These questions should make your prospect feel a problem is larger and more urgent than he or she may have initially thought. For example, your prospect may see hard-to-use internal software as just an annoyance, a necessary cost of doing business. Implication questions can help shed light on the problems caused by this hard-to-use software: does it lead to employee overtime because they struggle to accomplish things efficiently? Does it decrease overall quality of work? Does it impact employee turnover?

Each of the above questions helps frame the issue as a larger one in your prospect's mind. Then, you transition to the final set of questions.

5. **Need-payoff questions.** These questions focus attention on your solution and get buyers to think about the benefits of addressing the problem. Such questions should stem from the implication questions you asked earlier, and can include: *How do you feel this solution would help you? What type of impact would this have on you if we were to implement this within the next few months? Whose life would improve if this problem was solved, and how?*

The SPIN (Situation, Problem, Implication, Need-payoff) question model is a natural progression. First you clarify that the prospect is a potential customer and break the ice (situation questions). Then, you get them talking about the problem (problem questions). Next, you uncover all the implications of this problem (implication questions). Finally, you focus on how your solution addresses these implications and will solve their problem (need-payoff questions).

## Cold Calling

How do you get your first customers? As Steve Barsh, former CEO of SECA (acquired by MCI), said in our interview, "You get your first customers by picking up the phone." If you are fortunate, you may be contacting people you know or were introduced to warmly by a friend. However, you may have to get your first customers by cold calling or emailing prospects.

We interviewed Todd Vollmer, an enterprise sales professional with over 20 years of sales experience, who told us his approach to cold calling. Tactically, setting daily or weekly targets for outbound calls can help you get through the process. You'll be able to push yourself through some of those uncomfortable feelings (mainly stemming from rejections) with a concrete goal to work toward.

When making cold calls, be judicious about the people you contact. Cold calling junior employees is just as difficult mentally as calling more senior employees, but has a much lower success probability because they have less decision making authority and industry knowledge. Sean Murphy suggests that your first interaction should be with employees who have some power, but aren't too high up:

*"Ordinarily, it's somebody who is one level or two levels up in the organization; they've got enough perspective on the problem and on the organization to understand what's going to be involved in bringing change to the organization. As we work with them they may take us up the hierarchy to sell to more senior folks.*

*We don't tend to start at the top unless we are calling on a very small business, in which case you've got to call on the CEO or one of the key execs because no one else can make any decisions."*

Once you understand the potential first customer's problem and you think your solution can help solve it, you can start to focus conversations on closing the customer. Specifically, Todd recommends getting answers for five specific areas he calls PNAME:

**Process** – How does the company buy solutions like yours?

**Need** – How badly does this company need a solution like the one you're offering?

**Authority** – What individuals have the authority to make the purchase happen?

**Money** – Do they have the funds to buy what you're selling? How much does *not* solving the problem cost them?

**Estimated Timing** – What are the budget and decision timelines for a purchase?

After a successful first call, Todd suggests sending a follow-up email documenting what you talked about including the problems your prospect faces and the next steps.

He also suggests **closing emails with a direct question such as "will you agree to this closing timeline?"**

### Good First Customers

You'll want your first customers to have a problem they're actively looking to pay to solve. Unfortunately, many enterprise entrepreneurs do not put enough thought into deciding on their first customer. Identifying the wrong first customer can lead to wasted time and squandered resources. Sean Murphy shared some pitfalls to avoid when seeking out a first customer:

*"One [problem] occurs when the prospect invites you in... [but] has no interest in buying what you have or will develop. They would like to learn a lot about this emerging technology area, or this problem area, or something like that...*

*The second situation that's also a waste of time is when someone claims to be a "change agent." He will tell you that your offering is going to have a huge impact; it's going to transform all of General Motors, for example. Substitute your favorite lighthouse customer. Before you get started doing everything that he is telling you to do, you need to ask him, "Have you ever brought other technology into your company?" More often than not unfortunately he will say "Well no, but you know I've only been here six months, and this is what's going to let me make a big difference here."*

*So, the two typical problems are, you end up giving away free consulting or you talk to somebody that in their own mind is this change agent, but they have no idea how to make it happen."*

You also want your first customers to be somewhat progressive and willing to work with you closely. As you're still developing your product, you want their involvement in helping you craft the best solution.

As such, getting the right first enterprise customer is crucial, as it will inform many decisions about the importance of different features.

Forming this strong relationship is also crucial because you want to use your first few customers as references and case studies to give your startup some measure of credibility when you start designing your sales funnel.

## Designing a Sales Funnel

With a sales funnel you start with many prospects, qualify the ones that make good customers, and sell a certain number of them on your solution. We interviewed David Skok, partner at Matrix Ventures and five-time entrepreneur (he's taken three companies public and one was acquired), to talk about creating profitable sales funnels.

**Generating Leads**

The first goal is to drive leads into the top of the funnel. Usually, this means using other traction channels to make people aware of your product. While cold calling or emailing can be an effective way to reach your first customers, David believes it's less effective when trying to build a repeatable sales model:

*"I'm in favor of gaining traction through some kind of marketing channel first, then using sales as a conversion tool to close [those leads] into business. It's very, very expensive to use cold calling, and really not that effective by comparison with using marketing to get some kind of qualified prospect and then using sales to close that prospect."*

**Qualifying Leads**

The next stage in a sales funnel is lead qualification. Here, you want to determine how ready a prospect is to buy, and if they're a prospect in which you should invest additional resources. For example, many companies require an email address and some company information in order to access materials on their site (e.g. a whitepaper or ebook).

This information is then used to determine which prospects are worth spending more time on. For example, HubSpot, which sells $10k+ marketing automation software, uses this information to determine how much time they should invest in a lead. If they get a lead from someone running a small business on Etsy or eBay, they may choose to invest less time in that prospect because chances are someone running a side business part-time is not a good fit.

Mark Suster, two-time entrepreneur and partner at Upfront Ventures, suggests a simple approach to bucket leads into three categories: A's, B's and C's:

*"I define "A deals" as those that have a realistic shot of closing in the next 3 months, "B deals" as those that you forecast to close within 3–12 months and "C deals" as those that are unlikely to close within the next 12 months.*

*"A deals" should get much of the salesperson's time (say 66–75% of time), "B deals" should get the balance as each sales rep needs to build their pipeline and bigger deals take time.*

*And the key to scaling is that "C deals" should get no time from sales. They should be owned by marketing."*

In many organizations, marketing is in charge of generating leads and doing basic lead qualification. Then, the sales team further qualifies and eventually closes the leads. It is part of the marketing department's job to make sure the sales team gets the information they need to just focus on qualified leads. Mark has this to say about marketing and sales working together:

*"Marketing's job in working with salespeople is twofold:*

> *A. To arm – which means to give the reps all of the sales collateral they'll need to effectively win sales campaigns. This includes presentations, ROI calculators, competitive analyses, and so forth.*

*B. To aim* – which means helping sales reps figure out which target customers to focus on. It's about helping weed out the non-serious leads from the urgent ones."

## Closing Leads

Once you've qualified your leads, the final step is to create a purchase timeline and convert prospects to paying customers. Todd recommends laying out exactly what you are going to do for the customer, setting up the timetable for it, and getting them to commit (with a "yes or no") to whether or not they will buy.

An agreement at this stage might look like this: "We'll build this feature within two weeks. After two weeks, if you like the feature we've built and it meets your needs, you'll buy from us. Yes or no?" Getting a yes or no answer allows you to focus your time on deals that are likely to close without wasting time on prospects that aren't prepared to buy.

Closing leads can happen in a variety of ways. For some products, it can be done completely by an inside sales team (meaning salespeople that don't travel). This team usually calls qualified leads, does a webinar or product demo, and has an ongoing email sequence that ends with a purchase request. In other cases, you may need a field sales team that actually visits prospective customers for some part of the process – it all depends on the complexity and length of your sales cycle.

## Sales Funnel Strategy

Remember that, no matter how good your sales team, the customer is the one who decides to buy your product. It is crucial to keep the customer in mind as you design your sales funnel, meaning you should make their decision to buy an easy one. As David said in our interview:

*"You want to recognize that your prospect has a series of issues and questions they will want resolved before they make a buying decision. These are things like 'Am I sure that this is the best product?', 'Am I sure that this will work for my situation?', 'Will I get a good return on investment?', 'Will this integrate with a system I have working in place today?' and so on.*

*A lot of companies design their sales cycles around how **they** think things should work. I believe very strongly in the notion that you have to design it from the customer standpoint inwards, as opposed to your standpoint outwards, which is the normal way I see people thinking about this stuff.*

*Once you know what that buyer's questions are, you want to design your process to effectively address all of their questions and recognize what kinds of things need to be handled. Ideally, as many of these questions you can handle on your website, the better. Your job, once you have their email, is to answer all of their buying questions and then create a trigger that gives them a strong reason to buy"*

You can track when prospects drop out of your funnel. The points in your funnel where many prospects drop off are called **blockages**. Prospects will fall out of your funnel due to sales complexity; you want to make purchasing your product as simple as possible. Some ways you can minimize blockages are through:

- Removing need for IT installs with SaaS (Software as a Service)
- Free trials (including through open source software)
- Channel partners (resellers of your products)
- Demo videos
- FAQs
- Reference customers (such as testimonials or case studies)
- Email campaigns (where you educate prospective customers)
- Webinars or personal demos
- Easy installation and ease of use
- Low introductory price (less than $250/month for SMB, $10,000 for enterprises)
- Eliminating committee decision making

## Case Study: JBoss

JBoss, an open source provider of middleware software, created a sales funnel that drove $65 million in revenue just two years after founding (Red Hat later acquired them for $350 million).

JBoss first focused on generating leads. Over five million people had downloaded their free software through SourceForge (a popular open source software directory), but JBoss had no contact information for these prospects. Knowing they needed a way to consistently generate leads, they gave away their software's documentation (which they previously charged for) in exchange for a customer's contact information.

This worked out well because customers were motivated to get the software documentation, which showed them how JBoss worked. Contact information was a small price to pay. For JBoss, this information was crucial as they could now communicate with prospects about their paid offerings. This tactic generated over 10,000 leads per month.

That many leads are a problem of their own – it's nearly impossible to contact that many leads individually. It was now time for JBoss to qualify these leads and determine which were most likely to buy. They used Eloqua, a marketing automation software, to determine the pages and links a prospect engaged with before accessing the documentation. Prospects who spent a lot of time on support pages were good candidates for the JBoss support service – the product that generates revenue for the company.

JBoss's marketing team would call these promising leads to further qualify them. Each of these calls was made specifically to determine if a prospect had the desire to get a deal done. If so, qualified prospects were passed to sales.In this final stage of the funnel, prospects were contacted by individuals from an inside sales team. This is where the standard sales process kicks in: calls, demos, whitepapers, etc..

The sales team closed about 25% of these prospects thanks to their thorough lead qualification (industry averages hover between 7–10%).

Unqualified leads not yet ready for sales were put into lead nurturing campaigns. These prospects received the JBoss Newsletter, invitations to webinars, and were encouraged to subscribe to the JBoss blog. Customers who reached a certain level of interaction with nurturing campaigns (for example, those who clicked on certain links in emails or signed up for two webinars) would then be put back in the sales pipeline and contacted by someone from sales.

JBoss built an impressive and wildly successful sales funnel. A big reason for its success was that it was designed from the standpoint of their customer. They utilized free tools to generate leads at a low cost by offering customers the documentation they wanted. They qualified them through marketing built on customer education. Finally, they used an inside sales team to close each deal at an average deal size above $10,000.

## Takeaways

- Sales works best for high-priced products that require some customer hand-holding.

- Good first customers have a burning need to address a problem, are interested in your approach to solving their problem, and are willing to work with you closely.

- Cold calling should not be ruled out as a sales approach, especially when trying to find first customers.

- The goal of sales is building a repeatable sales model. An effective sales funnel has prospects enter at the top, qualifies these leads, and closes them effectively.

- To close sales effectively, get the buyer to commit to timelines based on specific actions being taken and met. At each point get an affirmative that you are on track to close.

- When designing your sales funnel, always keep in mind the perspective of the customer, especially in terms of reducing the complexity of the buying process.

See our sales resources and discuss this traction channel with us and other startup founders on our forum:

http://tbook.us/sales

# CHAPTER 19

# Affiliate Programs

An affiliate program is an arrangement where you pay people or companies for performing certain actions (like making a sale or getting a qualified lead). For example, a blogger may recommend a product and take a cut when there are sales through the blog. In this case the blogger is the affiliate. Companies like Amazon, Zappos, eBay, Orbitz, and Netflix use affiliate programs to drive significant portions of their revenue. In fact, affiliate programs are the main traction channel for many ecommerce stores, info products and membership programs.

For this channel, we interviewed Kris Jones, founder of the Pepperjam affiliate network, which was acquired by eBay in 2009. Kris grew Pepperjam to become the fourth largest affiliate network in the world:at one point, they had a *single advertiser* generating *$50 million* annually through their network.

## Common Affiliate Programs

Affiliate programs are frequently found in retail, information products, and lead generation.

**Retail**
Retail affiliate programs facilitate the purchase of tangible products and account for more than $2 billion annually. Amazon, Target, and Wal-Mart have the biggest programs and pay affiliates a percentage of each sale they make.

Amazon's affiliate program, for example, pays between 4–8.5% of each sale depending how many items an affiliate sells each month.

Some large retailers like Amazon and eBay run their own affiliate programs, but this is rare. These programs involve recruiting, managing and paying thousands of affiliates, which is too complex (and too expensive) for most companies. It is much more convenient for online retailers to go through existing retail affiliate networks if they want to use this traction channel.

Sites like Commission Junction (CJ), Pepperjam, and Linkshare all have strong networks of affiliates who make a living promoting others' products. The list of companies who take advantage of these networks contains the most recognizable names in the retail industry: Wal-Mart, Apple, Starbucks, The North Face, Home Depot, Verizon, Best Buy, and many others.

The affiliates that join these programs vary widely, but generally fall into the following major categories:

- **Coupon/Deal sites.** These sites (e.g. RetailMeNot, Coupon-Cabin, BradsDeals, Slickdeals) offer discounts to visitors and take a cut of any sale that occurs. For example, when you search for "Zappos discount," RetailMeNot is likely to rank highly for that search term. When you visit the RetailMeNot page that comes up, you get coupon codes for Zappos. If you click through and buy something using a code, RetailMeNot gets a percentage.

- **Loyalty programs.** Companies like Upromise and Ebates have reward programs that offer cash back on purchases made through their partner networks. They earn money based on the amount their members spend through retail affiliate programs. For example, if 1,000 members buy gift certificates to Olive Garden, Upromise will get a percentage, of every dollar spent. Then, they pay part of what they earn back to their members.

- **Aggregators.** These sites (e.g. Nextag, PriceGrabber) aggregate products from retailers. They often add information to product listings, like additional ratings or price comparisons.

- **Email lists.** Many affiliates have large email lists they will recommend products to, and take a cut when subscribers make purchases.

- **Vertical sites.** There are hundreds of thousands of sites (including individual blogs) that have amassed significant audiences geared towards a vertical (e.g. parenting, sports, electronics, etc.).

### Information Products

Information products include digital products like books, software, music, and (increasingly) education. Since it doesn't cost anything to make another digital copy, selling info products through affiliate programs is quite popular. Creators will give large percentages to affiliates that promote their products.

By far the largest affiliate network for information products is Clickbank, where affiliate commissions often reach 75%. ClickBank has over 100,000 affiliates and millions of products.

### Lead Generation

Lead generation is a $26 billion dollar industry. Insurance companies, law firms and mortgage brokers all pay hefty commissions to get customer leads. Depending on the industry, a lead may include a working email address, home address, or a phone number. It may also include more qualifying information like a credit score.

Affiliate programs are popular with financial services and insurance companies because the value of each customer is so high. Think of how much you spend on auto or health insurance annually: that should give you a sense of why a lead is so valuable. In fact, insurance companies are top Google AdWords spenders, often paying $50–100 for a single click!

These companies often create their own affiliate programs or go through popular lead-gen networks like Affiliate.com, Clickbooth, Neverblue and Adknowledge.

## Affiliate Program Strategy

**Your ability to use affiliate programs effectively depends how much you are willing to pay out to acquire a customer.** After all, with this channel you are paying out of pocket for the lead or sale.

### Using Affiliate Networks

We recommend going through an existing affiliate network – something like Commission Junction, Pepperjam, ShareASale, or a more specific networks targeted at your type of product. Using a network makes it easier to recruit affiliates (because so many are already signed up on these sites) and therefore allows you to start using this traction channel immediately. Otherwise, you'd have to first recruit affiliates on your own, which takes time and money.

Setting up an affiliate program on an existing affiliate network is relatively easy, though it requires an up-front cost. In the case of Commission Junction, that cost is over $2,000. If you successfully recruit high-performing affiliates already on the site, their sales will quickly cover the initial fee.

### Creating Your Own Affiliate Program

The other option is to build your own affiliate program independent of an existing network. With such a program, you recruit partners from your customer base or people who have access to a group of customers you want to reach.

One benefit of this approach is you don't have to pay your affiliates all in cash. Instead, you can use the features of your product as currency. For example, if your startup has a freemium business model you could give away certain features or extend subscriptions. In chapter 6 (on viral marketing) we explained how Dropbox's referral program involves giving people free storage space. Another example is QuiBids, a top penny auction site. They built out a referral program for their current users that gives free bids to users who refer other users.

## Affiliate Program Tactics

The first place to look for potential affiliates is your own customer base. They are easy to recruit and work with because they are already familiar with and (hopefully) like your brand.

After getting customers involved in your affiliate program, you will want to contact content creators, including bloggers, publishers, social media influencers and email list curators. Monetizing blogs can be difficult, so these content creators often seek other ways to make money.

We interviewed Maneesh Sethi, popular blogger at HackTheSystem, to talk about how companies can build relationships with people like him. Maneesh has been an affiliate for many products he's personally used, including a program that taught SEO tactics. He loved the program, so he contacted the company and worked out a deal with them to give him a commission for each new customer he sent their way. After agreeing to terms, Maneesh sent out an email to his list mentioning how the SEO program had helped him get better rankings on Google. That single offer has made him nearly $30,000 in two years.

Maneesh also has recommended RescueTime, a time-tracking application that helps you be more productive. As one of their top affiliates, he has referred over three thousand people to the product since he joined their affiliate program. Through Maneesh, RescueTime was able to reach a new audience without spending a lot of money on marketing or wasting it on leads that didn't convert.

Maneesh mentioned that the best way to reach someone like him is by building a relationship: help the content creator where you can, write guest posts, provide free access to your product, etc. In turn, they'll happily promote you if you have a truly great product.

**Compensation**

Well-established affiliate programs like those run by Amazon or Net-flix have figured out exactly how much to pay their affiliates for each lead. As a startup, you are going to be less sure of your underlying business and **should start with a simple approach.** The simplest approaches are to pay a flat fee for a conversion (e.g. $5 for a customer that purchases something) or pay a percentage of a conversion that occurs (e.g. 5% of the price a customer pays).

More established affiliate programs get more complex by segmenting products and rewarding top affiliates. eBay gives coupon codes to their affiliates for product categories they want to push. Tiered payout programs are also popular among larger programs. In this structure, affiliates get paid a percentage (or flat fee) of each transaction. The percentage is based on the number of sales you make – if you drive more transactions, your rate goes up, and you make more money.

## *Major Affiliate Networks*

Here are the top affiliate networks, as well as a list of software tools that can help you build your own referral program without a substantial engineering investment.

> **Commission Junction** – CJ has many of the largest Internet retailers on their platform. They are also somewhat pricey: it costs upwards of $2,000 to sell your product through their network. This high cost, combined with the fact that they curate both affiliates and publishers for performance, creates a high level of quality in their network.

> **ClickBank** – The leading platform for anyone selling digital products online (courses, ebooks, digital media).ClickBank is relatively cheap to start with, as you only need to pay $50 to list a product on their platform.

**Affiliate.com** – Affiliate.com promises a very strict affiliate approval process, which they claim means higher quality traffic for their advertisers.

**Pepperjam** – Started by Kris Jones (who we interviewed for this chapter), the Pepperjam Exchange encompasses multiple channels (mobile, social, offline retail, print, etc.). They promote their customer support and transparency as selling points for their network, which costs $1,000 to join.

**ShareASale** – This affiliate network has over 2,500 merchants and allows advertisers to be flexible in determining commission structures. It costs about $500 to get started.

**Adknowledge** – They offer traditional ad buying services in addition to affiliate campaigns. They also work in mobile, search, social media and display advertising, giving advertisers access to affiliate and CPC outlets through one platform.

**Linkshare** – They play in both the affiliate and lead generation spaces. They help companies find affiliates and build lead gen programs for them. Companies like Macy's, Avon, and Champion use them to manage affiliate programs.

**MobAff** – A mobile affiliate network that companies can use for both CPC and CPA. Mobaff utilizes SMS, push notifications, click to call, mobile display and mobile search to drive conversions for their advertisers.

**Neverblue** – Neverblue is targeted toward advertisers that spend more than $20,000 per month. They also work with their advertising partners on their advertisements and campaigns. They count Groupon, eHarmony, and Vistaprint are some of their clients.

**Clickbooth** – Clickbooth uses search, email, and many websites to promote brands like DirecTV, Dish Network, and QuiBids.

**WhaleShark Media** – This media company owns some of the most popular coupon sites in the world, including Retail-MeNot and Deals2Buy.com. Companies can partner with them to drive coupon-based affiliate transactions through their sites, which often appear near the top of Google for any "term + coupon" search.

## Conclusion

Kris stressed that more startups should take advantage of this traction channel. As he put it:

*"For startups that don't have a lot of money, where you can't just open a PPC (pay-per-click) account and start throwing darts, affiliate marketing seems to me to be a logical place to start.*

*There's really no guarantee on that if you spend 10k on Google AdWords you'll make more than that. If you were to compare affiliate marketing and PPC, the **advertiser** assumes the risk in PPC. If you set up poorly written and poorly thought out campaigns on AdWords, you're going to have to pay for the click whether or not your ads suck, or whether or not they're converting well.*

*With affiliate marketing, you get to define what the transaction or the conversion is, and you also have tools available to mitigate low quality. For instance, if someone refers an ecommerce transaction to you but the credit card is declined, the affiliate commission is zero.*

*If someone submits a lead form, but the lead doesn't follow the rules you set out (a legitimate email address, a real postal address, etc.), you don't have to pay for that. You don't assume the risk."*

## Takeaways

- An affiliate program is an arrangement where you pay people or companies for performing certain actions (like making a sale or getting a qualified lead). For example, a blogger may recommend a product and take a cut when there are sales through the blog.

- Affiliate programs are generally found in the retail, information product, and lead generation spaces and have been very successful specifically in financial, dating, web hosting, weight loss, and even poker spaces.

- Common affiliate types in retail are coupon sites, loyalty programs, aggregators, email lists, and niche sites.

- Your ability to use affiliate programs effectively depends how much you are willing to pay to acquire a customer. After all, you are paying out of pocket for the lead or sale.

- Using an existing affiliate network makes it easier to recruit affiliates (because so many are already signed up on these sites) and therefore means you can start using this traction channel immediately. Otherwise, you'd first have to recruit affiliates on your own.

- When you do look to recruit affiliates, the first place you should look is your current list of users.

See our affiliate programs resources and discuss this traction channel with us and other startup founders on our forum:

http://tbook.us/affiliate

# CHAPTER 20

# Existing Platforms

Existing platforms are websites, apps or networks with huge numbers of users – sometimes in the hundreds of millions – that you can potentially leverage to get traction. Major platforms include the Apple and Android App Stores, Mozilla and Chrome browser extensions, social platforms like Facebook, Twitter, and Pinterest, as well as newer platforms that are growing rapidly (Tumblr, Snapchat, etc.).

Zynga, a social gaming company, got much of their early traction by building games on the Facebook platform, where they focused on Facebook's sharing and friend-invitation capabilities.

Similarly, when mobile video-sharing app Socialcam launched, they suggested users sign up with Facebook or Twitter, promoted user videos on both platforms, and encouraged users to invite their friends from each site. They went on to hit 60 million users within 12 months – that type of growth just isn't possible through many other channels.

## App Stores

With the number of smartphone users well above one billion and growing every day, we've seen an explosion of apps reaching millions of users in short periods of time: months, rather than years.

### App Rankings and Features

The most efficient way for an app to get discovered in the App Stores is through the top app rankings and featured listings sections.

These rankings group apps by category, country, popularity and editors' choice. The story of Trainyard illustrates the impact an App Store feature can have.

Trainyard, a paid iOS game developed by Matt Rix, wasn't growing the way he had hoped. Since free applications are downloaded at a much higher rate than paid, app developers will often release a free version and monetize those free users via in-app purchases or paid upgrades.

Matt decided to try this tactic. When he released the free version of Trainyard (Trainyard Express), an editor at a popular Italian blog wrote a glowing piece on it almost immediately. This propelled the app to the #1 free app in Italy – netting over 22,000 downloads on that day alone! The app then hit the top spot in the UK and was downloaded over 450,000 times in a week. Then this happened:

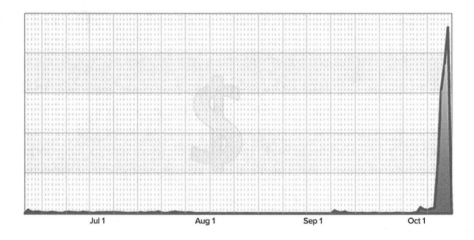

Just seven days after Matt launched Trainyard Express, Apple decided to feature it. The graph above shows what it looks like when your app is featured on the main page – it completely blows up.

**Ranking Strategy**

Trainyard illustrates the importance of getting enough attention for your app so that it shows up in the rankings. Mark Johnson, founder of Focused Apps LLC, wrote about how app promotions usually work:

1. *Ads get the [app] somewhere into the charts*

2. *Now it's in the charts, more people see it*

3. *So it gets more organic downloads*

4. *Which makes it go a bit higher up in the charts*

5. *Now even more people see it and it gets more organic downloads*

6. *People like it and start telling their friends to get it too*

7. *It goes up higher in the charts*

8. *Repeat from 5*

Companies use a myriad of tactics to get into the charts initially. They buy ads from places like AdMob, buy installs from companies like Tapjoy, cross-promote their apps (through cross-promotion networks or other apps they own), or even buy their way to the top of the charts through services like FreeAppADay.

Other traction channels can also drive adoption of your mobile app: as Trainyard showed, the PR and targeting blogs channels can work well. While none of these tactics are enough on their own, they can help you get the ball rolling towards a ranking or feature.

**Compelling Apps**

For top rankings to happen sustainably, you need to have a compelling app that is rated highly on a regular basis.

Ratings matter a lot – they influence individual choices to download an app, editors choose apps to feature based on them, and they're often mentioned in any press coverage.

There are some tricks you can use (like asking users to rate your app right after you give them something useful), but really the base experience has to be excellent to get consistently high rankings. Even with hundreds of thousands of apps, there are shockingly few that are truly amazing user experiences. Most of the apps that are now household names – Instagram, Path, Google Maps, Pandora, Spotify – all have excellent user experiences and consistently high ratings.

## Social Platforms

The use of social sites is constantly shifting as people change where they communicate online. Newer social platforms like Snapchat and Vine are adding users at a dizzying pace, and we're sure others will follow them soon.

Even though keeping up with the evolution of social platforms can be challenging, they remain one of the best ways to rapidly acquire large numbers of users. In fact, it makes sense to focus on platforms that are just taking off.

Social platforms that haven't fully matured also haven't built all of the features they'll eventually need; you might be able to fill in one of those gaps. They also are less saturated, as larger brands are often slower to target up and coming sites.

### Filling Gaps

YouTube got its initial traction by filling gaps in the MySpace platform. In the mid-2000s MySpace was the most visited social networking site in the world. Video sharing on the web wasn't user friendly – it was difficult to upload videos and put them on other sites.

MySpace didn't have a native video hosting solution. YouTube provided one that was simple: you could upload and embed a video in MySpace in a matter of minutes.

Even better for YouTube, MySpace users were directed *back* to You-Tube when they clicked on the embedded videos. This exposed many MySpace users to all of the great features and content available on You-Tube, and was responsible for YouTube's rapid early growth.

Every major platform has similar stories. Bit.ly fulfilled the need to share shortened links on Twitter and saw most of their adoption from such users. Imgur built their image-hosting solution for reddit users, and has seen an explosion in usage as a result. This pattern repeats itself time and time again.

## Add-ons and Extensions

Browser extensions (in Chrome) and add-ons (in Firefox) are apps you can download for your web browser. The most popular browser extension is Adblock Plus, which blocks ads on major websites. Other popular extensions help you download YouTube videos, save book-marks across computers, and save your passwords.

There's a reason add-ons are such a popular way to spur growth. Web users visit dozens of different sites every day; to establish yours as a site they consistently visit can be difficult. An add-on allows users to get value from your product without consistently returning to your site.

Evernote, a memory-enhancement and productivity tool, saw a huge jump in users when they launched their browser extensions. In their 2010 Year in Review blog post, they said web usage went up 205% thanks to their extensions – and this from a company with over 6 million users at the time!

Like App Stores, browser extensions have sites to download the apps, though they are all free. These sites have features and rankings, which you should be similarly seeking if you focus on this area.

## Other Platforms

There are thousands of other large sites and marketplaces that you can target to get users. First, figure out where your potential customers hang out online. Then, create a strategy to target users these existing platforms. Sites like Amazon, eBay, Craigslist, Tumblr, GitHub, and Behance have all helped startups build traction.

AirBnB saw much of their early growth come through Craigslist. Customers who used Craigslist found that AirBnB was a much simpler and safer solution. With this knowledge, the company's engineers developed a "Post to Craigslist" feature that would allow you to list your bed on Craiglist. Though it eventually shut down this feature, it drove tens of thousands of Craigslist users back to AirBnB to book a room.

PayPal, the leading online payments platform, used a similar strategy when they targeted eBay users as their first customers. In the beginning, PayPal itself purchased goods off of eBay and required that the sellers accept their payment through PayPal. This worked so well that PayPal proved more popular than the payment system eBay itself was trying to implement! This single-minded focus allowed them to acquire a large percentage of users within one of the few groups of buyers and sellers that dealt with payments on the early web.

## Case Study: Evernote

Since its founding, Evernote has focused on existing platforms as their main traction channel. We talked with Alex Pachikov, one of the founders of Evernote. His company was recently valued at over one billion dollars.

### The Build-Early Strategy

Evernote has made it a priority to be on every new and existing platform. They benefit from the platform's initial marketing push and increase their chances of getting featured. As their CEO, Phil Libin, puts it:

*"We really killed ourselves in the first couple of years to always be in all of the App Store launches on day one. Whenever a new device or platform would come out, we would work day and night for months before that to make sure Evernote was there and supporting the new device or operating system in the App Store on the first day... When iPhone launched we were one of the very first iPhone apps, so we were promoted and had a lot of visibility.*

*When iPad launched, we were there on day one, not just with a port of our iPhone client, which a lot of other companies did ... [We had] a completely new designed version for the iPad even though we'd never seen an iPad before – we stood in line with everyone else. Same thing with Android devices and the Kindle Fire."*

Being first can open you up to the opportunity to benefit the early marketing and promotion about the platform itself. As Alex said:

*"Every year there's a new platform, new device, new something, and as somebody who's starting a company you should consider if there's something really cool you can do on an upcoming platform. Now obviously you can't plan if a platform is going to be successful, but you can [make some] reasonable guesses based on past experiences with a company.*

*I think people see this as gambling. People take the 'I will support this platform when it has a million users' type of approach. That's a fine thing to do if you are EA or Adobe or something like that. And maybe for Evernote a year from now, that's the right thing to do. But for a startup, you really aren't in that position. When a platform is popular, it's crowded... A lot of people have cool apps and could do really, really well if they were to get this initial push, and that initial push is free if you do it early. But you risk that all that effort is a waste."*

Evernote was one of the first apps available for Android. Because they had some very cool functionality, they were featured in the Android store for six weeks at a time when it was far less crowded than it is now. This gave them hundreds of thousands of new users, all because they were early and focused their engineering efforts on being first on the platform. Similarly, when Verizon picked up Android phones, Evernote benefitted from the national marketing push Verizon did to promote their Android launch.

This build-early strategy doesn't work in every case, especially when the underlying platform flops. Evernote took the same approach with the Nokia, Windows, and Blackberry smartphone platforms, none of which moved the needle. Nevertheless, Alex is very happy with the overall strategy: when it works – like with Android – it more than makes up for the failures.

**Multiple App Strategy**

In the last few years, Evernote's strategy has been to expand beyond their pure note-taking app and release many different apps for specific verticals (Evernote Food for food notes, Evernote Hello for remembering people, etc.). **Since getting promoted in App Stores has been their most effective growth tactic, this strategy enables Evernote to get featured and ranked in categories where Evernote's main app does not appear.**

**Special Features Strategy**

At Evernote, Alex mentioned they think hard about what types of features or apps would stand out to editors:

*"You have to think ahead. What types of things would Apple or Google really like? What are things that, if we were to do, Apple or Google or Microsoft would be looking for? And is there a natural fit between what we do and what they would be looking for?"*

This thought process leads to apps like Evernote Peek. Peek is an app that allows you to turn your media (notes, videos, or audio) into study material that you interact with using the iPad Smart Cover. It feels magical and it took advantage of a new Apple technology at the time. It was so cool that Apple itself showcased it in a commercial!

Peek was featured in Apple's Education category, and was the #1 Educational app for over a month. This exposure led to over 500,000 new Evernote users who experienced the product through Peek, and was one of the strongest growth drivers for the company during that year.

## Newer Platforms

Though Evernote has seen most of their growth come through mobile channels, their platform strategy works perfectly well on non-mobile platforms. The important takeaway is that it is a good idea to focus on new and untapped platforms to generate growth. Chris Dixon, a partner at Andreessen Horowitz and the founder of Hunch before its acquisition by eBay, had this to say about platform-based growth:

*"Some of the most successful startups grew by making bets on emerging platforms that were not yet saturated and where barriers to discovery were low...*

*Betting on new platforms means you'll likely fail if the platform fails, but it also dramatically lowers the distribution risks described above."*

## Takeaways

- Step one is to figure out where your potential customers are hanging out online. They could be on major platforms, on niche platforms, or some combination. Then you can embark on a strategy to target these existing platforms.

- Existing platforms include the iPhone and Android App Stores, the Firefox and Chrome browser extension stores, social platforms such as Facebook, Twitter, and Pinterest, and other newer platforms that are gaining traction every day (Tumblr, Foursquare, etc.).

- If you focus on one of the stores, your goal should be to get high rankings or featured. For that to happen sustainably, you need to have a compelling app that is regularly rated highly.

- Large companies have been built on the back of each major social platform by filling gaps with features that the platform was not providing itself.

- A tactic that has been successful is to focus on new and untapped platforms, or new aspects of major platforms because there is less competition there.

See our existing platforms resources and discuss this traction channel with us and other startup founders on our forum:

http://tbook.us/platforms

# CHAPTER 21

# Trade Shows

Trade shows are a chance for companies to show off their products in person. These events are often exclusive to industry insiders, and are designed to foster interactions between vendors and their prospects.

Early on, you can use this traction channel to build interest in (and demand for) what you're building. As you get more established, you can use trade shows as an opportunity to make a major announcement, sell big clients, seal a partnership or as an integral part of your sales funnel.

We interviewed Brian Riley of SlidePad Technologies, the company behind the SlidePad bike brake. His startup has used trade shows to gain traction at every phase, from pre-product to a major distribution deal with a large bike manufacturer. We also spoke with Jason Cohen, founder of WPEngine, who used trade show marketing at his first company, Smart Bear Software.

## Picking Trade Shows

Almost every industry has large number of trade shows: the tough part is deciding which ones to attend. **The best way to decide whether to attend an event is to visit as a guest and do a walkthrough the year before.** Attending as a guest allows you get a feel for an event without straining your budget.

If this isn't possible, the next best option is to get the opinions of people who have attended previous events – *how crowded was it? How high was the quality of attendees? Would you go again?* These are important questions that will help you decide if an event is right for your startup.

Brad Feld, a partner at Foundry Group, suggests following these steps when deciding which events to pick:

1. Set your goals for attending trade shows this year. For example, are you trying to get press, lure investors, land major customers, work out significant partnerships, or something else? Your goals should drive your decisions about which events to attend and how to approach them.

2. Write down all events in your industry.

3. Next, evaluate each event in the context of your goals. In particular, think about the type of interactions you want and whether these interactions take place at each event. For example, if you need to have long conversations with prospects to do customer development, seek out an event with an intimate atmosphere. If your goal is to interact with as many potential customers as possible, a crowded event would be a better fit.

4. Figure out how much you can spend per year and allocate this budget by quarter. This allows you to align events on your schedule with your budget while also giving you flexibility to reallocate in later quarters if company goals change.

5. Finally, work backwards to see if attending a particular event makes sense given your quarterly budget. For example, let's say you are attending Traction Trade Show and your goal is to increase sales. When you receive the attendee list from the conference organizer (ask for it if it is not provided), you see that 10,000 people are going. However, only 30% of those people fit the profile of a potential customer, so your total number of people to target is 3,000 people.

If it will cost you $10,000 to attend this trade show and the price of your product is $5,000, it may make sense for you to attend. That is, your trip will be profitable around the third sale with these numbers, so then the decision comes down to what other opportunities you have right now. However, if you are selling a $50 product, you probably won't sell enough to make attending this trade show worth your while.

SlidePad attended a few trade shows early on with prototypes on hand – no manufacturing line, no pricing, and no plans to sell anything. Their goal was simply to have conversations with other companies about the features they wanted to see in SlidePad's products.

From these conversations, they learned what their product needed from a technical standpoint and the price points they needed to hit. Later, when they had developed a product, they increased their presence (and expenses) at trade shows. In other words, as their company goals changed, their actions at each show changed with them.

## *Preparing for Trade Shows*

**Your preparation for a trade show will determine how successful you will be.** This is one of the few times during the year where nearly everyone in your industry is in one place; you'll want to be at your best.

To prepare, make a list of key attendees you want to meet at the trade show. Then, schedule meetings with them **before you attend the event**. Brian sent well-researched emails explaining what SlidePad did and how their technology could benefit the people he wanted to meet. He also attached a one-pager with more information about the company. This strategy allowed him to meet the people he wanted at every event he attended.

Jason Cohen put it this way:

*"Set up meetings. Yes, meetings! Trade shows are a rare chance to get face time with:*

- *Editors of online and offline magazines. Often overlooked, editors are your key to real press. I've been published in every major programming magazine; almost all of that I can directly attribute to talking with editors at tradeshows! It works.*

- *Bloggers you like, especially if you wish they'd write about you.*

- *Existing customers.*

- *Potential customers currently trialing your stuff.*

- *Your vendors.*

- *Your competition.*

- *Potential partners.*

*Proactively set meetings. Call/email everyone you can find. It's easy to use email titles which will be obviously non-spam such as 'At [Trade Show X]: Can we chat for 5 minutes?' I try to get at least 5 meetings per day. Organizing dinner and/or drinks after the show is good too."*

If PR is one of your goals, reach out to media that will be in attendance. Media members attend trade shows *specifically* to see what's going on in an industry – give them something to write about! This could be a new product, feature or deal with a big customer.

Successful trade shows come down to the relationships you build and the impression you make on journalists, prospective customers and potential partners. Mark Suster, partner at Upfront Ventures, also suggests hosting dinners for people at events:

*"The other secret conference trick that is orchestrated by the true Zen masters is to schedule a dinner and invite other people. It's a great way*

*to get to know people intimately. Start by booking a few easy-to-land friends who are interesting. Work hard to bag a "brand name" person who others will want to meet. All it takes is one. Then the rest of your invites can mention that person's name on the guest list (name others, too ... obviously) and you will be able to draw in some other people you'd like to meet.*

*Another similar strategy is with customers. If you invite 3–4 customers and 3–4 prospects to a dinner with 2–3 employees and some other interesting guests you'll be doing well. Potential customers always prefer to talk to existing reference customers than to talk to just your sales reps.*

*Final tip: picking a killer venue is one of the best ways to bag high-profile people. Everybody loves to eat somewhere hot. However, sometimes a dinner can be too expensive for an early-stage company. So why not go in on the dinner with two other companies? That way you're all extending your networks and splitting the costs."*

## Trade Show Tactics

First, determine where you want to be located on the show floor. If your goal is to reach many attendees (as opposed to targeting a few high-value prospects), you need visibility. That means you want a booth in a well-trafficked location and a marketing plan to get people to take notice. If your strategy is dependent on talking to just a few key partners, a great booth location (and the added cost that comes with it) doesn't make as much sense. In fact, you may want to be situated in a very particular place (say next to a specific company).

No matter what your location, you will want to put together an impressive display. Having a big banner that says what you do, nice-looking booth materials (tables, backdrops, etc.), business cards, and a compelling demo are the basics. If that seems like a lot to put together, there are many vendors that help companies create trade show materials.

To attract people to their booth, Jason Cohen, founder of Smart Bear Software, would send out discount cards for their software to all attendees before the actual conference. The recipients had to come to his booth to redeem the discounts.

Giveaways (t-shirts, pens, etc.) are also a way of getting some buzz and inbound traffic at a trade show. Coffee mugs and stress balls are tried and true, but you can get even more creative with more unique items (yo-yos, coconuts, cigar lighters) to stand out during the show.

You can also be proactive on the trade show floor to bring people back to your booth. The founders of RJ Metrics, a business analytics subscription service, told us about how they've had success starting conversations by walking up to people at trade shows:

*"One thing was clear: it pays to have an outbound strategy. Only 28% of our conversations were walk-ups. This means that employing an outbound strategy allowed us to extract between 3 and 4 times as much value from the show as we would have otherwise."*

Many companies do something particularly engaging within their booths to get people to stay there long enough to experience their full pitch. SlidePad has a funny video demo comparing their brakes to the regular brakes found on bikes. The video shows an individual using regular bike breaks speeding down a mountain and braking, then getting thrown promptly over the handlebars. Then, as a comparison, the same person in the same scenario brakes using a bike with Slide-Pad brakes and comes to a quick, safe stop. It's a funny way to pique people's interest in their product: then, they can follow up later with more information and steer prospects towards their goal.

When you do engage a person, each of the materials you give out should have a specific call to action (CTA). For example, if someone picked up a business card at your booth, it should have a compelling offer (e.g. download a free industry guide), along with a unique link to that download (e.g. http://yoursite.com/tradeshow). Make sure this page is mobile optimized, as most of your visitors will be accessing the page from a mobile device. Having a CTA lets you track how many people from the show went to your unique page and adds a few people to your email list.

**Outside The Booth**

There's more to a trade show than the trade show floor. In many cases, one of your primary goals will be building relationships. Getting to know potential customers and partners in a social setting can get you more traction than you'd expect.

We already talked about hosting dinners. David Hauser, the founder of Grasshopper, mentioned that he schedules at least one dinner for Grasshopper customers at every event they attend. One step beyond dinners is throwing a party near the show center. Like dinners, these are a great way to loosen up and chat with others at the event. You could co-sponsor these with other startups to keep costs reasonable.

## Conclusion

Trade shows give you more direct interaction with customers, partners, and press in a short period of time than most other traction channels. This channel has the potential to move the needle in a matter of days.

That's what happened with SlidePad. After a major industry trade show, they managed to form a relationship with Jamis, one of the largest players in the bike manufacturing industry. They met Jamis early on, when they had just a prototype. From that meeting, SlidePad learned the necessary specifications they'd need to have if they wanted to work with Jamis.

After SlidePad built their product to those specs, SlidePad formed a manufacturing relationship with Jamis. Their brakes are now stopping thousands of bikes nationwide, and is their biggest source of traction. And all of it started and grew through this traction channel.

## Takeaways

- The ideal way to decide whether you should exhibit at a trade show is to visit as a guest and do a walkthrough the year before. The next best option is to get the opinions of people who have attended the event in previous years.

- Your traction goals should drive your decisions on which events to attend. For example, are you trying to get press, lure investors, land major customers, work out significant partnerships, or something else?

- Schedule meetings with people you want to meet at trade shows (e.g. potential customers, partners, press) well before you attend the event. Dinners are a great way to combine meetings.

- Have an inbound and outbound strategy for your booth. Structure the inside of your booth (including what you say) around your particular goals. Include a strong call to action on every item (e.g. business card) you give out.

See our trade shows resources and discuss this traction channel with us and other startup founders on our forum:

http://tbook.us/shows

# CHAPTER 22

# Offline Events

Sponsoring or running offline events – from small meetups to large conferences – can be a primary way to get traction. Twilio, a tool that makes it easy to add phone calls and text messaging to applications, attracted its customers by sponsoring hackathons, conferences, and meetups large and small. Larger companies like Oracle and Box throw huge events (Salesforce's Dreamforce conference has over 100,000 attendees!) to maintain their position as market leaders.

In phase I, offline events give you the opportunity to engage directly with potential customers about their problems. Such events are especially important when your target customers do not respond well to online advertising or do not have a natural place to congregate online. Attracting these customers to one location or going to a place where they meet in person can be the most effective way to reach them.

Offline events are particularly effective for startups with long sales-cycles, as is often the case with enterprise software. We'll look at how Enservio reached decision-makers and shortened their sales cycle by using this channel. On the other end of the spectrum, you can use offline events to build relationships with power users, as both Yelp and Evite have done successfully.

## Conferences

Conferences are the biggest and most popular type of offline event. Each year hundreds of startup-related conferences and thousands of business conferences are held worldwide.

You can benefit from a conference in any startup phase. In phase I, where smaller groups of people can move the needle, attending meet-ups and events is a prime way to do so. Startups in phase II can take advantage of larger tech conferences like TechCrunch Disrupt, Launch Conference, and SXSW to build on their existing traction. Twitter launched nine months before SXSW in 2007 and was seeing decent amounts of traction, on the order of several thousand users. Because many of their early users were headed to SXSW, Twitter saw the conference as an opportunity to accelerate their adoption. As Evan Williams, Twitter's co-founder said:

*"We did two things to take advantage of the emerging critical mass:*

1. *We created a Twitter visualizer and negotiated with the festival to put flat panel screens in the hallways… We paid $11K for this and set up the TVs ourselves. (This was about the only money Twitter's \*ever\* spent on marketing.)*

2. *We created an event-specific feature where you could text 'join sxsw' to 40404. Then you would show up on the screens. And, if you weren't already a Twitter user, you'd automatically be following a half-dozen or so "ambassadors," who were Twitter users also at SXSW. We advertised this on the screens in the hallways."*

Thanks to this conference-specific marketing, Twitter jumped from 20,000 tweets per day to 60,000+ by the end of the conference. Twitter also won the SXSW Web Award, leading to press coverage and even more awareness of their service.

## Your Own Conference

Eric Ries wanted to broaden the audience for the lean startup principles he was promoting on his blog. However, he was afraid his message would get lost at a large conference like SXSW. Instead, he organized his own conference and invited founders of successful companies to talk about how lean principles worked in their startups.

First, Eric tested demand for his conference by asking his readers if they would be interested. After a resounding yes, he sold conference tickets through his site and other popular startup blogs.

Startup Lessons Learned began as a one-day conference in San Francisco with just a few speakers and panels focused on Lean Startup concepts. The short event was attractive to individuals who didn't want to spend a lot on travel or take time off work. In addition, Eric avoided the extra cost and coordination headaches that come with arranging a multi-day event: flying in speakers, hotel stays, and so on. In short, he made the commitment to attend as simple as possible. The result was a strong turnout and a great conference experience.

The Startup Lessons Learned conference was about promoting Lean Startup ideas. While he didn't want people to have to travel to attend, he still wanted people from out of the area to find out what was happening at the conference. To this end, Eric live-streamed the conference to meetup groups across the country. The people that attended those meetups (or watched on individual live-streams) were instrumental in promoting his ideas to a larger audience and making his book a bestseller.

Other companies have built traction by holding more lavish affairs. This was the case with Enservio, a company that sells expensive software to insurance companies. Enservio was struggling to reach top executives in the insurance industry through other traction channels – sales, business development and SEO weren't working.

To get traction, Enservio went all out to organize the Claims Innovation Summit. They held it at the Ritz Carlton in beautiful Dove Mountain, Arizona, for multiple days. They made sure not to make the event feel at all like a sales pitch for their services. Instead, they pulled in prominent figures from major consulting firms, respected individuals in the insurance industry and founders of hot startups to come speak. They then used this group of speakers to attract the industry executives that were their prospective customers. Not only could the executives learn from the speakers, but they could network and vacation at the same time.

The event successfully attracted top decision-makers and established Enservio as an industry leader overnight. They've now established this conference as annual event in their industry.

MicroConf is a smaller conference for self-funded startups that attracts hundreds of founders and sells out in days. It is run by Rob Walling of HitTail. When Rob first started MicroConf he had difficulty attracting people to a conference they'd never heard of. As he said:

*"We struggled to sell tickets [for the first MicroConf]... I ran Facebook ads and did [Google] AdWords, but neither really worked. Anything that wasn't relational, where people hadn't heard of the conference, didn't get traction... We also put together an ebook with quotes and articles from some of MicroConf's speakers where you had to pay with a tweet to get it. It went pretty viral, but didn't sell any tickets.*

*Some people said it was too expensive. I think for some people that was an issue, but I think it comes down to being able to prove value. Since it was unproven, they just didn't know if they were going to spend that $500, plus airfare and hotel, and it would just be a crappy or mediocre conference. Once the first year proved itself, suddenly people were saying we need to raise the price – people have no issue with the price now."*

Rob spoke about the types of companies that have the potential to benefit from meetups and other offline events:

*"Companies with customers who have shared interests, who have a kind of community or at least a need for one, I think that's the type of company that will benefit most. I don't know that HitTail would be a good example of a company that could throw a good conference...*

*Our customers are all over the board (real estate, doctors, startups, etc.), so throwing an SEO conference probably wouldn't be all that helpful.*

*Any niche where the market is online and easily reachable would be a good one, because everyone wants to go to a conference. Any niche where you have recognizable names you can go after would also be good."*

## Meetups and Smaller-Scale Events

Instead of a conference, you may choose to connect with a target group of customers at a meetup. For example, if you're a small SEO software company, you might hold a meetup where you discuss the latest and greatest SEO tactics.

Small meetup groups are more effective than you may expect, especially in the early stages. Seth Godin used meetups when launching his book *Linchpin* he organized Linchpin meetups in cities all across the country through his blog. In total, more than 10,000 people attended these events, where they connected over ideas that Seth wrote about and built relationships with each other.

Great meetups can create lasting community connections. The meetup groups that watched the livestream of the first Lean Startup conference continues to meet years after: over twenty cities still have regular "Lean Startup Circle" meetups. These events allow practitioners to continue to connect over the ideas in Eric's book; they've also helped keep Eric's book on the bestseller list.

You can start your own meetup, join an existing one, or even sponsor an event where your prospective customers will be. Meetup.com is the most popular site for doing so.

Nick Pinkston, founder of automated manufacturing startup Plethora Labs and the Hardware Startup Meetup group, saw a need for a community around the budding hardware startup movement. In the Bay Area there were hundreds of events and meetups focused on software startups, but not a single one focused on the unique needs and challenges of hardware startups.

Nick organized his first meetup at TechShop SF. The first meeting drew 60 people and the only expense was $70 for pizza. An event like this makes for a great test case given how easy it is pull off. In Nick's case, there was lots of interest from attendees – the group now has more than 2,600 members.

## *Party!*

Believe it or not, throwing a party can be an effective way to get some traction. Evite did this when they helped stage one of the largest parties in the Bay Area for Internet celebrity Mahir Cagri. The party was one of the premier social events of the year, and Evite was responsible for organizing and sending out all invitations.

This event exposed Evite to their target customer in a memorable manner. Who doesn't want a party invite? Attendees were then likely to use Evite when throwing their own parties.

Yelp had a similar experience when trying to jumpstart usage in new cities. They would throw parties where Yelp Elites (their term for top Yelp users) were allowed to RSVP first, given free food and swag, and treated like VIPs.

When other users heard about or such perks, it gave them an incentive to be more active on the site.

## Offline Event Tactics

### Starting Out

Although MicroConf has become a huge event, Rob suggested that **a day-long mini-conference could be a great way for a smaller startup to get traction.** It can also be an easy and cheap way to test if there's any interest among your audience for a larger event.

For example, you can select a topic relevant to your product and invite the founders of three local companies to come give short talks on the subject. You could also feature these founders on a panel about a particular topic. You might even take the unconference approach and have attendees suggest topics for roundtable discussion, and then allow them to vote on which discussions will take place.

A local university lecture hall is a good place to hold an event like this. Often, universities are willing to open their facilities if it's for an educational purpose and if some of their faculty or students can attend. This type of mini-conference can be done for less than $500.

### Scaling Up

If your first event is a success, consider scaling up to larger events. The logistics of planning a larger event will take a lot more effort because you need more of everything (speakers, food, space, etc.). Sponsors may be interested in helping you cover the cost of the event. For MicroConf, companies with products built for startups offset the cost of putting on the conference. Consider this: the price for two lunches and snacks at the hotel where Rob held the first MicroConf was $26,000! That's a lot of money, especially at a conference that intentionally restricts the number of people who can attend.

Rob also made a few key points about creating a great event. **Keeping attendee quality as high as possible is crucial** so that those who attend the conference will learn a great deal from both the speakers and from other audience members. Rob has found the best way to do this is to make the ticket price relatively high, so that individuals with successful businesses are more likely to attend than those just starting out.

The structure of an event also plays a critical role in whether the experience works for you and the attendees.

With MicroConf, Rob intentionally keeps it small so that attendees have a chance to meet everyone else at the event and the speakers could get to know the attendees. At larger events, speakers get mobbed after they give a talk or sit on a panel. At smaller events, each attendee can connect with every speaker personally. Rob facilitated these conversations by having the speakers sit with the attendees at lunch and participate in roundtable discussions.

## Conclusion

If you are creative and willing to try something different, throwing a successful event can be a big win. One of the reasons offline events are effective is that so few startups are doing them. As Rob said:

*"I think the overarching thing for marketing is [startups] need to try more things, and fail faster and more quickly... Trying all of this stuff and seeing what works is paramount. The tried and true approaches like Facebook and AdWords are so crowded now.*

*People need to think about doing things that don't scale. Early on when you're trying to get those first 1,000 customers, you have to do things that don't scale. You have to take more risks.*

*You can still build a business without being creative. If you don't have creativity, you need money. You need one or the other."*

## Takeaways

- Conferences are the biggest and most popular type of offline event. Launching at a conference has been a successful phase I conference tactic.

- If there isn't a conference that directly brings together your target customers, consider starting your own.

- You can test this channel by attending a couple conferences or hosting a few smaller meetups or a one-day mini-conference.

- Throwing parties, either alongside conferences or across many cities, is another successful strategy to attract and reward prospective customers. Similarly, meetups can be a scalable tactic to build local communities in cities around the world.

See our offline events resources and discuss this traction channel with us and other startup founders on our forum:

http://tbook.us/events

# Speaking Engagements

In the previous two chapters, we touched on speaking at trade shows (chapter 21) and offline events (chapter 22). In this chapter, we will discuss how to land these speaking engagements and how to make them compelling.

It's relatively easy to get started in this channel – simply start by giving free talks to small groups of potential customers or partners. Speaking at small events can improve your speaking ability, give you some early traction, and spread your story or message. It's also good for personal growth if you've never done it before: Mark Zuckerberg has talked about how improving at public speaking has vastly improved his management ability. Therefore, we recommend trying to give at least one talk even if you choose not to pursue this traction channel.

Dan Martell is the founder of Clarity, an advice platform that connects founders with successful entrepreneurs. He spoke to us about getting traction through speaking engagements:

*"Speaking is funny. You know to me, it's the old school concept that teaching sells... Teaching is what content marketing is all about: webinars, blog posts, and the like. I look at [these] things as the future of good marketing. The opportunity to teach and be in front of a room for 45 minutes introducing your company and your story to potential customers is time well spent."*

This channel works well wherever there are a group of people in a room that – if you pitched them right – would move the needle for your business. This happens to occur more with enterprise and B2B businesses because they're often at expensive conferences, though Dan has gotten traction from talks he's given for Clarity (a consumer-focused platform).

## How to Land Speaking Engagements

**You have to get the attention of event organizers to land speaking engagements.** Event organizers *need* to fill time at their events. If you have a good idea for a talk and see an event that aligns with an area of your expertise, simply pitch your talk to the event organizers. If your ideas are solid, they will want you. This process becomes even easier as you become a recognized expert.

### Pitching Talks

Steve Barsh (a serial entrepreneur and former CEO of PackLate) has successfully pitched conference organizers to present many times. Rather than pitch them directly on what he wants to talk about, he contacts them and asks them about the ideal topics they want to have speakers cover at an event. Once known, he then crafts the perfect pitch: one that hits on key points the organizers want to cover.

To determine where you want to speak, make a list of the events in your industry. Different kinds of events have different crowds and different expectations of speakers. There are a few types of events you should be aware of:

- Premier events are well regarded and attended national or international shows. Often, there will only be a few of these per year in an industry. These events will require much longer lead times to submit a proposal, often six to twelve months.

- Regional events bring together industry players within a day's drive. Depending on the event, expect to land a speaking engagement roughly two to four months before the show.

- Local events draw city residents around a particular topic. Like regional shows, lead times can vary but are usually one to three months before the show.

Organizers consider timing, topic, and credibility when selecting a speaker. By establishing yourself as an expert on an appropriate topic and submitting proposals far in advance, you maximize your chances of securing one of the best speaking engagements at the target show.

Landing speaking engagements is *far* easier if you have expert credentials. After all, if you don't "earn the right" to be on stage, the audience wont' give you the attention you deserve. For example, if you run a popular blog, it becomes much easier for organizers and attendees to find and recognize your expertise. In Dan Martell's case, he had done a lot of social marketing with Flowtown (his first startup), which gave him the credibility to land his first major talk.

**Building Your Speaking Reputation**
In addition to industry experience, conference organizers will want to see that you are a decent speaker. If you're not well known as a speaker, they'll be hesitant to book you (even for free)

Getting valuable early speaking experience is not difficult. **Start by speaking for free at co-working spaces, nonprofits, and smaller conferences or events.** Use these smaller scale appearances to refine your talks and build your speaking reputation.

The world of event organizers is relatively small and they pay special attention to who is speaking at events. As a result, you'll find your number of engagements growing organically. As Dan told us:

*"To become a speaker you have to speak once. If you speak and you're good, people in the audience will ask you to speak at other events. That's just how it happens. I've never marketed myself as a speaker; it's not in my bio or anything. What happens is, you speak at a conference, people see it or talk about it, and you get invited to other ones."*

If you do a good job at smaller events, leverage them into talks at larger events by asking for referrals and using past gigs as social proof.

## Speaking Tactics

When you start a talk, the audience is usually thinking about two questions – *why are you important enough to be the one giving a talk? What value can you offer me?* These questions will be burning in their minds until you address them, so answer them immediately. For this reason, Dan told us he does his own introductions and talks to highlight how he started and sold his two previous companies (Flowtown and Spheric) for millions.

Once you've captured the audience's attention, keep it with a compelling story. All successful talks tell a story: otherwise, the audience loses interest. Your story is about *what* your startup is doing, *why* you're doing it, and specifically *how* you got to where you are. In Dan's case, he talks about how he started Clarity after he got so much great advice at his previous startups.

Of course, we have only so many compelling stories. That's why Dan gives the same one or two core talks, only slightly modifying each to fit the audience. He never does custom talks and always reuses his slides, so his two speeches are solid:

*"I usually figure out who are two target customers that I want to reach, because it's hard to give more than two good talks. For Clarity, it's entrepreneurs and potential partners. Try to figure out the two tracks your potential customers might be interested in and try to teach them about that. For us, it's helping entrepreneurs get great advice and how it's changed my life, so I have a talk about my entrepreneurial journey and why getting the right advice can change your life."*

Giving a limited number of talks is helpful in another way: it gives you more practice per talk, which helps you identify spots that may not be clicking with the audience.

**The more practiced and comfortable you are, the better your talks will be and the more you can improve them.**

## Advanced Tactics

If you want to focus speaking engagements, we spoke with Dan about a few more advanced tactics you can use.

**Leveraging Your Talks**
Record your speaking engagements. If you're at an event of 250 people and you have given your best speech ever, you've still only reached 250 people. However, if you can record your best speech ever, you can post clips, thereby exposing your story to thousands of people who would never have seen it otherwise. Among this group will be conference organizers who will book you for future events.

Leveraging social media to reach people *outside* of the conference is a similar tactic. Rand Fishkin of Moz tweets his slides before every presentation, which lets his followers find out what he'll be talking about. Then, when he posts a video of his talk, there is already some buzz and interest in hearing what he talked about.

Dan will even try to leverage social media *during* his talk. He asks for the audience's "divided attention," meaning he wants them to tweet and share good content from his presentation as he gives it. To facilitate this, he includes his Twitter handle on every slide and asks people to tweet at him if they really identified with something he said. This way, he can find out the content his audience enjoyed the most, while also growing his reach.

On top of asking his audience to tweet and text, Dan also gives the audience a call-to-action at the end of his presentations. This is a simple request of the audience – something like asking them to sign up to a mailing list or to check out a link where they can see his slides. This tactic tells him whether or not members of the audience found the information engaging enough to act on it.

## Reusing Slides

We already mentioned that Dan only prepares two talks that he delivers at speaking engagements. But, what if one conference asks for a twenty-minute presentation and another asks for sixty? It's time-consuming to prepare a whole new talk: it's more efficient to tailor your existing slides to a specific audience or event. As Dan said:

*"The best talks I've ever seen are where each slide is essentially a 7 minute story with a beginning, middle, and end. Once you get good at that, and you have these canned slides, you can change a 60 minute talk to a 20 minute talk just by taking slides out."*

The slides for your presentation are an important part of any talk you'll give. Every slide in your presentation should be engaging. We've provided several great resources on making compelling visuals on our discussion forum.

## Building Relationships

As we mentioned early on, the main driver for being a speaker in the first place is to build relationships. At most conferences there is a speaker's dinner, where presenters get to meet each other and network. If there isn't one scheduled, Dan usually takes the liberty of scheduling one. Often, this can be the most valuable part of a conference – you get to meet other individuals doing cool things.

Similar to trade shows, you can also do preparation ahead of time based upon who is likely to attend the event where you are speaking. Get a list of attendees from event organizers and reach out to people you would like meet. Tell them exactly when and where they are speaking and suggest to meet up afterwards. Now that they've heard you talk they'll be more receptive to your pitch.

## Conclusion

Because speaking engagements are good for personal growth, we recommend trying to give at least one talk even if you choose not to pursue this traction channel. Doing so is also a good test for whether this channel can drive traction for your company. It is one of the few channels that can quickly cement your place in an industry. If you give the right talk at the right time to the right people, it can make you a respected industry leader overnight.

## Takeaways

- Remember that event organizers need to fill time at their events. If you are a fit for their event, then you are doing them a favor by presenting.

- Organizers consider timing, topic, and credibility when selecting a speaker. By establishing yourself as an expert on the right topic and submitting proposals far in advance, you maximize your chances of securing one of the best speaking engagements at the target show.

- The world of event organizers is relatively small, especially within a given topic, and they pay attention to who is speaking at events in the field.

- Most successful talks tell a story on stage. Without a story, the audience will lose interest. We suggest telling a story that tells what your startup is doing, why you're doing it, and specifically how you got to where you are.

See our speaking engagements resources and discuss this traction channel with us and other startup founders on our forum:

http://tbook.us/speaking

# CHAPTER 24

# Community Building

Community building involves investing in the connections among your users, fostering those relationships and helping them bring more people into your startup's circle.

You probably know people who won't stop talking about how helpful Yelp is for choosing a restaurant, or how awesome TripIt is for planning travel. These people are known as evangelists – passionate users who tell others about how awesome a product is.

Maybe after hearing about Yelp from your friend for a third time, you used the app yourself when looking for a dinner spot on Saturday night. Then, you found it so useful that you too became a Yelp evangelist. That is a direct example of how evangelists spread the word about a product and help build its community further.

We interviewed the founders of reddit, Wikipedia, Stack Exchange, Startup Digest, and Quibb to tell us how they created, grew, and nurtured their communities.

## How to Build a Community

### Build an Initial Audience
Every individual we interviewed emphasized how helpful it was to have an existing audience to jumpstart their community-building efforts. For example, Wikipedia began with a small group of users from the Nupedia user group (an earlier online encyclopedia project).

Stack Exchange is a network of high-quality question-and-answer sites, the most famous being Stack Overflow. Joel Spolsky and Jeff Atwood founded the company in 2008. Both were already "Internet famous:" Joel as the founder of Fog Creek Software, and Jeff as writer at codinghorror.com.

Thanks to their well-trafficked blogs, Jeff and Joel presented their ideas for Stack Overflow to readers who gave them feedback before the site launched. They even had the community vote on the *name* for Stack Overflow, and received nearly 7,000 submissions!

While this illustrates the power of an existing audience, it is an atypical startup experience. Few startups manage to get 7,000 users after 6 months, much less 7,000 votes on the name of a site that doesn't even exist. However, having an audience is not a prerequisite for building a successful community.

Chris McCann started Startup Digest by emailing twenty-two friends in the Bay Area about local tech events. As the list grew, Chris started giving twenty-second Startup Digest pitches at events he attended. His pitches proved effective: membership grew into the low thousands in a matter of months. Today there are over 250,000 members of the Startup Digest community, and it all started with those 22 friends.

**Establish Your Mission**
People want to feel like they're part of something bigger than themselves: that's why you **need to have a mission if you want to build an awesome community**. A powerful mission gives your community a shared sense of purpose and motivates them to contribute. As Jeff Atwood said:

*"We had a manifesto, and an idea of what we wanted to accomplish. And people bought into the vision because it was about them being awesome... [It is] about creating something that helps everyone in material and specific ways. It helps you get better at your job, at something you love doing. There was an idealism that people bought into with Stack Exchange, and we were out there talking about it all that time."*

## Foster Cross-connections

From our interviews we discovered that it's *critical* to foster connections among your community (through forums, events, user groups, etc.). By encouraging your users to connect around your startup, they feel more cohesive as a community and can come up with ideas that you may not think of yourself. Jeff said that failing to allow cross-connections was his biggest mistake in building Stack Overflow:

*"When people ask me what our biggest mistake was in building Stack Overflow I'm glad I don't have to fudge around with platitudes. I can honestly and openly point to a huge, honking, ridiculously dumb mistake I made from the very first day of development on Stack Overflow... I didn't see the need for a Meta.*

*Meta is, of course, the place where you go to discuss the place. Take a moment and think about what that means. Meta is for people who care so deeply about their community that they're willing to go one step further, to come together and spend even more of their time deciding how to maintain and govern it. So, in a nutshell, I was telling the people who loved Stack Overflow the most of all to basically ... f\*\*k off and go away."*

You can probably guess that every current Stack Exchange site launches with a Meta: a place where users can discuss how they can make the community better.

People who care enough about your startup's mission to discuss with others are your coveted evangelists. They are the people you want to support in every possible way.

## Communicate with your Audience

Community members love to hear from other members. But, they would also love to hear from *you*. You will want to connect with your evangelists and let them know that you value them.

In reddit's early days, any individual that wrote about reddit would get an email from Alexis Ohanian (the founder), thanking them for their writing. Alexis also sent shirts, stickers, and other gifts to early users.

He went so far as to coordinate an open bar tour for redditors, where redditors connected (and drank) on reddit's dime.

Sending emails and gifts is great, but nothing beats personal interaction. It's just easier to form a lasting relationship with someone you're sharing a laugh or a drink with. In that way, community building works nicely with other channels like offline events (see chapter 22) and speaking engagements (see chapter 23). These occasions present great opportunities for users to connect with you and with each other.

**Be Transparent**

Being open with your community is the best way to get them to buy into your mission. Jeff and Joel solicited feedback every step of the way, and built the site their community wanted. When Stack Overflow launched, their audience was already excited and had shaped the direction of the site. This resulted in hundreds of users in the first days, and thousands during the first month.

**Ensure Quality**

The meaning of quality depends on the service the startup provides. For Yelp, it might be the accuracy of its reviews; Wikipedia, the usefulness of its articles; reddit, the relevance of its links and comments.

Stack Overflow wanted to create the best question and answer site for developers – a community that truly helped developers get better at their jobs. Upon launch, Jeff established strict guidelines (decided on in tandem with the community) so that only practical, answerable questions would be allowed. Then he placed these guidelines on the Stack Overflow FAQ.

Since these community guidelines were prominently featured on the site, users often policed the site on their own – even more aggressively than Jeff himself would have. Not only did this keep quality high, but it kept members of the community engaged and invested in the future of the site.

Every founder we talked to emphasized the importance of maintaining community quality. Wikipedia developed strict guidelines for everything from the types of articles to include on the site to how conflicts of interest should be handled. Startup Digest focused on content selected by community members in each of its cities. Quibb uses an invite-only model to recruit people who they feel would be a positive addition to their community. Like Stack Overflow, reddit developed a karma system based on voting that determines what links and comments are displayed prominently.

Unfortunately, a common occurrence is that the quality of communities starts out strong but gets diluted over time as evangelists either leave or get drowned out by newer community members. This decline in the overall quality of the community causes more good people to leave, which creates a downward spiral from which many communities don't recover. To prevent this negative cycle, it is important **to focus on quality early on and set standards that can be maintained as the community grows**.

## Community Benefits

In addition to the obvious benefits from evangelism, your startup's community will have other benefits.

**Building Assets**
Many communities are a valuable asset for the managing company or organization. Consider Wikipedia: their goal is to compile the world's knowledge in one place. To reach this goal, they've built the largest group of knowledge contributors and editors ever assembled.

Other startups like Yelp and Codecademy have built core groups of users to accomplish their company goals. Yelp would be nothing without restaurant reviews from their users; many of Codecademy's programming lessons are user-generated as well.

Both sites have worked to attract users to their vision (Yelp's to allow people to discover their neighborhoods; Codecademy's to teach the world to code), and have thrived by leveraging their users to help accomplish that vision.

**Product Development**
Like building an asset, your users can also help you develop your actual product. Not only does this kind of community improve your product, but they will love you for giving them the chance to help.

Perhaps this community type is best illustrated by the open source movement. For software companies, their code is the product. Some companies open source their code, making it freely available for anyone to use, modify, or improve.

Tom Preston-Warner, founder of popular code hosting site GitHub, points out that open sourcing code generates free advertising and a lot of goodwill. GitHub is beloved by developers everywhere because they allow anyone working on an open source project to use GitHub free of charge. This drove a lot of their early adoption: when a developer wanted to work on a side project, GitHub was the first place that came to mind.

**Inbound Hiring**
Communities are excellent for recruiting and hiring. Everyone working at Gabriel's startup DuckDuckGo was a member of the DuckDuckGo community first. He calls this *inbound hiring* because everyone comes *in* from the community.

People that come from your community already buy into your mission. These are people you really want on your team, especially early on when you need to focus on shared vision to get through the inevitable ups and downs of a startup. You can also get a sense for what prospective employees can accomplish as individuals and community members before hiring them.

Finally, you are almost by definition hiring people that get things done. After all, these are community members that didn't just believe in your mission, but also took the initiative to help you achieve it.

## Conclusion

Chris McCann (of Startup Digest) talked about the types of companies that will benefit from community building:

*"I think building a community can be your traction. This is no small thing: it can truly get to crazy proportions on its own. That being said, there are definitely products and services that don't lend themselves to community building. If I were doing something with advertising and retargeting, it might be hard to build a community around that.*

*There are some businesses that lend themselves to doing this very well. Companies whose core function is the connecting of people are best set up to take advantage of community. Whether that's a trade show thing, an investment thing, whatever: when a company's underlying value is in bringing people together, and where people matter in the system, that's where this community stuff can really take off."*

## Takeaways

- Key to a strong community is cultivating and empowering evangelists. You also want to foster cross-connection among evangelists and community members in general (through forums, events, etc.).

- It is important to focus on community quality early on and set standards that can be maintained as the community grows. You can build tools and processes into your community (e.g. karma systems, rules) to help your community police itself.

- Community building can give you traction by magnifying your essential purpose, building a core asset, creating evangelists for your service, contributing to product development and even giving you a hiring pool.

See our community building resources and discuss this traction channel with us and other startup founders on our forum:

http://tbook.us/community

# CHAPTER 25

# Afterword

Thank you for reading the book! We've spent more than four years conducting over forty interviews, researching tons of additional material and synthesizing it all into more than 100,000 words. If you think this book was long now, our first draft was more than 50% longer!

All in all, we hope that you now have an actionable plan for getting traction. We've covered all nineteen channels you can use, a framework – Bullseye – to hone in on the channel that's most likely to move the needle for you, and a framework – Critical Path – for doing so.

Go forth and get traction!

Gabriel and Justin

yegg@duckduckgo.com

justin@justinmares.com

## Acknowledgements

First, we want to thank everyone who shared their traction stories and tips with us. Without you this book would not be possible:

- Jimmy Wales, Co-founder of Wikipedia
- Alexis Ohanian, Co-founder of reddit
- Eric Ries, Author of The Lean Startup
- Rand Fishkin, Founder of Moz
- Noah Kagan, Founder of AppSumo
- Patrick McKenzie, CEO of Bingo Card Creator
- Sam Yagan, Co-founder of OkCupid
- Andrew Chen, Investor in 500 Startups
- Dharmesh Shah, Founder of HubSpot
- Justin Kan, Founder of Justin.tv
- Mark Cramer, CEO of Surf Canyon
- Colin Nederkoorn, CEO of Customer.io
- Jason Cohen, Founder of WP Engine
- Chris Fralic, Partner at First Round Capital
- Paul English, CEO of Kayak
- Rob Walling, Founder of MicroConf
- Brian Riley, Co-founder of SlidePad
- Steve Welch, Co-founder of DreamIt
- Jason Kincaid, Blogger at TechCrunch
- Nikhil Sethi, Founder of Adaptly

- Rick Perreault, CEO of Unbounce
- Alex Pachikov, Co-founder of Evernote
- David Skok, Partner at Matrix
- Ashish Kundra, CEO of myZamana
- David Hauser, Founder of Grasshopper
- Matt Monahan, CEO of Inflection
- Jeff Atwood, Co-founder of Discourse
- Dan Martell, CEO of Clarity
- Chris McCann, Founder of StartupDigest
- Ryan Holiday, Exec at American Apparel
- Todd Vollmer, Enterprise sales veteran
- Sandi MacPherson, Founder of Quibb
- Andrew Warner, Founder of Mixergy
- Sean Murphy, Founder of SKMurphy
- Satish Dharmaraj, Partner at Redpoint Ventures
- Garry Tan, Partner at Y Combinator
- Steve Barsh, CEO of PackLate
- Michael Bodekaer, Co-founder of Smartlaunch

Each of you played a critical role in shaping this book and making it a useful resource. We'd also like to thank our early readers for their helpful comments and feedback, as well as Michael Zakhar and Brian Spadora for their editing help. Additional thanks to Eve Weinberg for pulling together the cover and Chris Morast and Doug Brown for making a beautiful website and book.

To Andrew Warner of Mixergy: your introductions and help throughout the whole process, set the tone for the book and gave us momentum and a plan in the early days when we were just starting to tackle this project.

To all the founders, investors and others who have published blog posts, resources and other tips that we've used in this book, thank you. We hope this book helps you in the same way your resources have helped us.

On a personal note (from Justin), thank you to my parents Kim and Peter Mares for your support and love throughout this process. Without you this book never would have happened.

Similarly (from Gabriel) thank you to my wife Lauren and the superhero kids Eli and Ryan.

## Discussion Forum

Join the conversation about Traction on our community forum, http://tbook.us/discuss.

Our discussion forum has a section for each traction channel. If you come across a great new post on a channel or would like to share your particular thoughts and experiences (especially tips, tricks, and traps), please share them on the discussion forum.

Similarly, please visit the forum and tell us about your traction journey. We'd love to hear from you and will have a community to support you in your pursuit of traction.

Finally, sign-up for our email list at http://tractionbook.com/. We'll be sending out resources and examples of successful applications of Bullseye and Critical Path, as well as new channel strategies and tools to help you get, keep and measure your traction progress.